"It's hard to talk about Saltie. Too easy to dismiss it as merely a sandwich shop. In a time when broad, white plates smeared with science and dotted with masculine, dildoic bravado are considered high art, Saltie makes the heroic plea for serving the common man an elemental, delicious food borne out of decades in the best kitchens in New York. I can't think of a more unintentional subversive act or a more profound work of love than the pleasure of a Saltie sandwich. You're my heart. I love you."

—TOM MYLAN

"Caroline Fidanza and crew have done something special at Saltie: taken a small mountain of finely-tuned, well-tested, and well-loved recipes that would put any restaurant on the map—as they did when Ms. Fidanza ran Diner—and distilled out frip and finery. What she and her partners offer between these covers (and at Saltie) is a roster of dishes so much more generous, more delicious, and more intelligent than any other 'sandwich cookbook' that it feels almost cheap to call it that. But that's what it is, and its modest, welcoming, and inspiring approachability help it stand out in the chef's cookbook crowd. The stories are good reading, the kitchen wisdom is actually wise, and the recipes scream 'COOK ME.'"

—PETER MEEHAN, co-editor *Lucky Peach* journal

Sandwiches

THE CAPTAINS DAUGHTER
LITTLE CHEF
SCUTTLEBUTT
SPANISH ARMADA
SHIPS BISCUIT
CLEANSLATE

ROMAINE DINGHY
BALMY

Saltie

Saltie

A COOKBOOK

by Caroline Fidanza

with Anna Dunn, Rebecca Collerton, and Elizabeth Schula

Photographs by Gentl & Hyers

CHRONICLE BOOKS

SAN FRANCISCO

Text copyright © 2012 by Caroline Fidanza.
Photographs copyright © 2012 by Gentl & Hyers.
Illustrations copyright © 2012 by Elizabeth Schula.

Library of Congress Cataloging-in-Publication Data available.

ISBN 978-1-4521-0302-0

Manufactured in China

Designed by **VANESSA DINA**
Prop and food styling by **REBECCA COLLERTON, CAROLINE FIDANZA, ELIZABETH SCHULA**
Typesetting by **DC TYPE, SAN FRANCISCO**

10 9 8 7 6 5 4 3 2

Chronicle Books LLC
680 Second Street
San Francisco, California 94107
WWW.CHRONICLEBOOKS.COM

Sandwiches

THE CAPTAINS DAUGHTER
LITTLE CHEF
SCUTTLEBUTT
SPANISH ARMADA
SHIPS BISCUIT
CLEANSLATE

ROMAINE DINGHY
BALMY

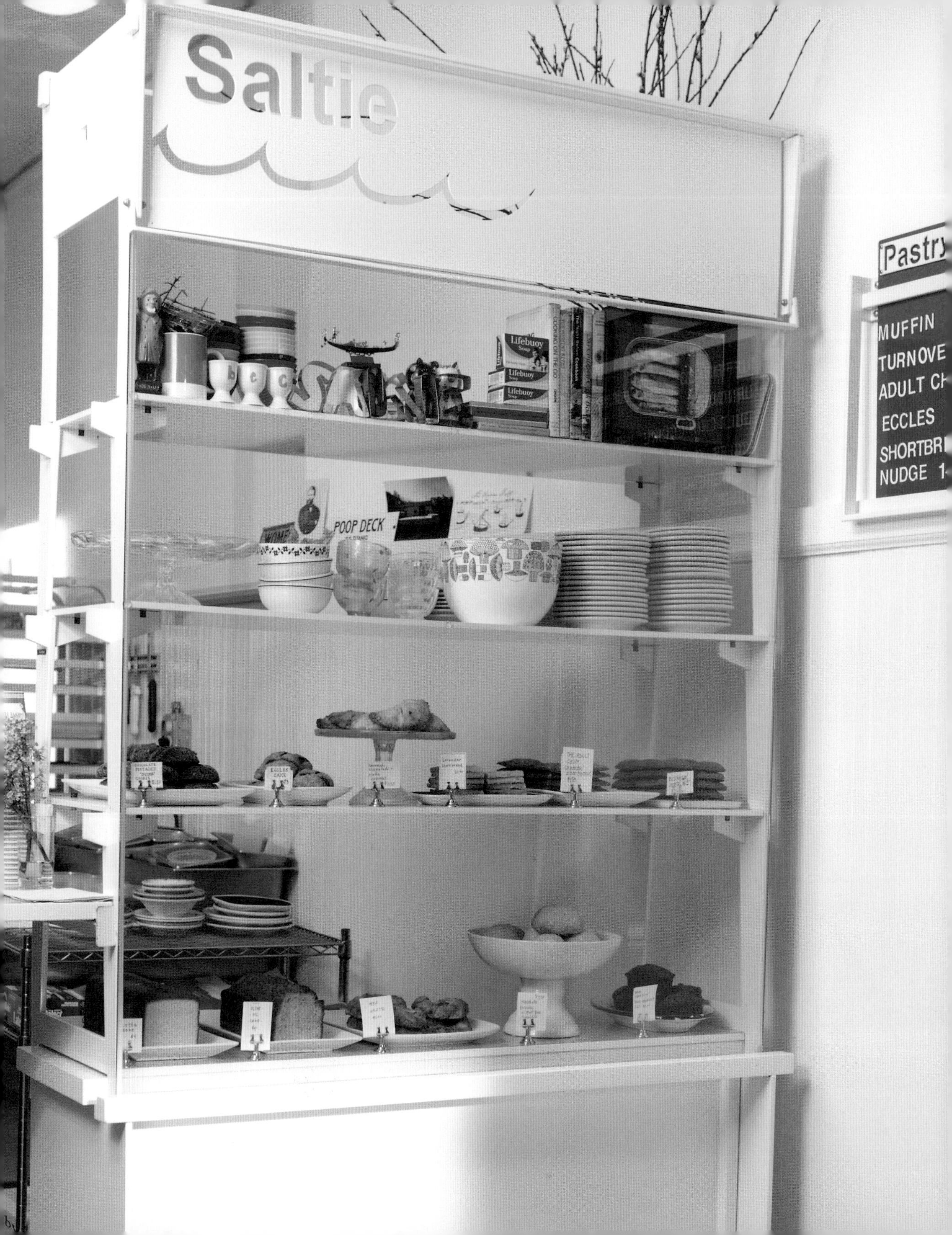
Saltie
Lifebuoy Soap
POOP DECK
Pastry
MUFFIN
TURNOVE
ADULT CH
ECCLES
SHORTBR
NUDGE 1

Saltie:

1. A saltwater **crocodile**—the largest, and perhaps most fearsome, living reptile on the planet.

2. A mammoth seafaring **vessel** that travels across the great Atlantic Ocean and through the St. Lawrence Seaway System to the Great Lakes. The ship arrives at Port Duluth in early April to pick up wheat and ferry it back across the ocean to Italy. A tiding of spring.

3. One tiny **sandwich shop** in Williamsburg, Brooklyn. At the whim of the season; a lesson in impermanence. Open ten to six, six days a week. A tight ship. A place for ideas and friends, a shoebox theater. Three women/chefs/friends searching for a kitchen and inspired by the great American novel _Moby Dick_ set out to create a bakery with strong coffee and a stronger imagination and found the finite and the infinite. The sea in a grain of salt.   —AD

CONTENTS

CONTINUED

CONTENTS

September 19 2010

I, <u>Mallicent Melissa Souris</u>,
Mallicent Melissa Souris

do hereby pledge my love &
devotion to Saltie & the ladies
and Rebecca, of said establishment

valid in continental USA & all the
allegedly other continents.

Herman Melville

PREFACE

The Peak of a Wave

by Anna Dunn

Amplitude. It's not hard to feel full in Brooklyn. Here, where a community of shimmering characters has seemingly sprung from cracks in the sidewalk, there is rarely a dull or colorless moment. The ground seems always to be gently roiling with the endless tides of creativity. This energy flows on the crescendo of a piano being keyed, the notes drifting from an open tenement window, wafting down onto the truck-packed streets. From the hum of sewing machines, the timbre of computer keys gently clacking, the soft scratch of ink on paper. This aliveness crests in one tiny blue-and-white kitchen down on Metropolitan Avenue.

I first met Caroline, Elizabeth, and Rebecca working the coffee counter on weekend mornings at Marlow & Sons, the now acclaimed restaurant tucked just under the Williamsburg Bridge and a stone's throw from the East River. At the time, I was employed weekdays at an independent bookstore in the city, running coat check at a salsa night on the Lower East Side, and trying to start my own small publishing company. I took the job making cappuccinos on weekends to make sure I could cover rent. It wasn't pretty. But I was young—and when you're twenty-five it is the very untenable and untamable nature of New York City herself that you desire. Nothing more. Nothing less.

I am not a morning person, so sprinting the eight blocks to Marlow at 6:00 A.M. was always a heart-pounding blur: across the park, over the Brooklyn-Queens Expressway, under the bridge, around the corner, and down the hatch into the warm, white-and-silver, sweetly pungent bakery. *Finish buttoning shirt; make sure belt is looped; straighten hair; run past baker; do not look up at clock; get up back staircase; start to set up shop. . . .* For the rest of the ten-hour day, at least in the beginning, I watched people come and go. I began to get a feel for the circadian rhythms of a day in the life of a restaurant and to glimpse for the first time what it is that makes a restaurant a kind of perfect vortex in the great cosmos of life. The rituals, the characters, the kaleidoscope of colors and aromas, the grace of spring, the ease of summer, the emptying of fall. Desire and fulfillment. I knew nothing of food.

My initial encounters with the Saltie trio were unique in that they were private. That is, these moments were truly my own, not shared even with the ladies themselves. I admit: I was terrified of them, perhaps as all youths are when they can sense they are in the company of greatness.

They called her Cheffie. When Caroline Fidanza entered the building, around one or two in the afternoon, rosy cheeked and feeling perhaps momentarily Zen, there was a palpable electrical shift in the air. Everyone wanted her ear, her adoration, her respect. It didn't take long for me to gather that she was the spiritual and intellectual Yoda, the den mother and the Demeter of this swath of handsome, hardworking, burgeoning food professionals. Not that Cheffie would ever let on. The nickname was almost more than she could allow. She would linger at the pastry counter in those early days, maybe to listen to Tom Mylan yammer on about whatever obscure Japanese knife or food curio had caught his ever-enthusiastic eye that week, or to quietly consider a cup of coffee, usually deciding against it but never denying its appeal. Then, down to the basement: chef's whites, clogs, a Sharpie and some torn butcher paper for notes, a trip through the walk-in, and the day began.

That considering she lent so graciously to the cup of coffee seems to me, in fact, to be the genesis and catalyst of Caroline's genius. The synapse-like attention to understanding a thing, any thing, for what it is in all of its varieties and innate and natural glory, informs her specific and brilliant kind of creativity. Whether we are at Guy Jones's farm, standing among the Brussels sprout stalks, ankle deep in loamy Hudson Valley black soil; at the dinner table of a crowded,

clattering Manhattan restaurant; or huddled in the warm glow of Saltie's prep station, I've seen it time and time again. Caroline will pause, sometimes just for a split second, sometimes prolonged, to discover the nature of whatever it is she is faced with and decide how best to honor it. A spiny artichoke, the ubiquitous egg, a piece of bread.

Later in the afternoon, Rebecca would grace us with her presence. She lived in the apartment above Marlow, and around two o'clock, she'd come straight from tumbling out of bed, her hair somehow perfectly pompadoured, the first cigarette of the day waiting only on that first sip of coffee. I was completely enamored of her English accent, her tattoos, and her cool. I was nervous. I blushed. Never have I ever enjoyed an insult as much as the one served to me on a slow weekday afternoon when Rebecca finally leaned over the counter and asked me to answer a crossword puzzle question. I'm pretty sure the clue had something to do with poetry, but I went blank. I must have mustered something utterly wrong; she was almost speechless with her disappointment in me. Rebecca straightened up, placed a Camel Light between her lips, smiled, and said, "I thought you were meant to be clever." This genuine nonchalance is at the very core of the wild integrity of Rebecca.

Determined, methodical, inspired, Rebecca slices scallions perfectly, painstakingly juliennes radishes and carrots only to garnish a striking bowl of soup. Rebecca, it seems, has a deep understanding that beauty is in the details. The architectural loft of lettuce towering on a plate. Pickles, yogurt sauce, our fresh herb mix, aioli . . . these are all her domain. She has within her the power to harness the tumultuous storm of a full-tilt restaurant kitchen while never straying from the path of precision, of perfection. Ahab and his White Whale: Rebecca and the Scuttlebutt (page 92).

Elizabeth has a true baker's temperament: one of attention to detail, focus, and an acute understanding of whatever medium she is working in. She has the mind and patience to repeat a task in exactly the same way every day, to make meaning out of method. When Elizabeth burst up out of the Marlow kitchen one afternoon, her kind blue eyes piercing through a white billow of sugar and flour, I felt an overwhelming sense of calm and immediate camaraderie. Here was a true sage. Her roles at Marlow & Sons and at Diner were nebulous, forever changing and vital. Line cook, baker, illustrator. It wasn't until we worked together on *Diner Journal* that I knew the great scope of her talents. Around the editorial table, after the scones had cooled, the crêpes had all been greedily consumed, and the flour was back on its shelf, we would toss around design ideas and motifs. The next week, without fail, Elizabeth—or, as we call her, Schula—would show up with something she had just been "playing around with." The unveiling would always reveal the most exquisite and delightful expression of watercolor, charcoal drawing, sculpting, stitching, etching, or sketching. Elizabeth's work exceeds expectation. She's a healer, an herbalist, and a naturalist, whether fermenting pickles, conjuring kombucha, or tending to the myriad plants in her garden. As a result, she has an extremely calming influence on the people around her. An effortless pioneer, she has roots deeply planted in the land and the art of living off it. She has a uniquely bright and exhaustive understanding of and reverence for the natural world.

It seems somehow disproportionate that these three forces of nature converged to inhabit one so small kitchen on one cloudy corner of the world. Saltie is a place of inspiration first and everything else second. A sandwich shop, a kitchen, a vision in blue and white, yes. But I have never made a visit to Saltie that didn't include bumping into a handful of people I love, all calmly attacking a sandwich of their choosing. I often wonder if one's choice of Saltie sandwich might in fact offer some insight into the fathomless depths of one's personality. But I keep these musings to myself. I have never felt so lucky and unconcerned as I do there, in the front window, reading the morning paper or catching up with a beloved friend, while unabashedly drooling *pimentón* aioli down my chin. No matter what the day holds—a wedding, a funeral, the winding car ride home—it is in everyone's best interest to stop by Saltie on the way. Somehow Caroline, Rebecca, and Elizabeth have managed to capture in food, in design, and in spirit that which puts the soul at ease. The shop lilts with life. And it is their relentless respect for life that makes whatever the Saltie trio creates flourish. I have been blessed over the years to carry on in concert with them: a pirate, a mystic, and a queen.

ROBERTSON

TARTINE BREAD

CHRONICLE BOOKS

The NEW SPANISH TABLE

BEYOND NOSE TO TAIL

VON BREMZEN

WORKMAN

VEFA'S KITCHEN

200 curries

An Invitation to Indian Cooking Madhur Jaffrey

Harvard Common Press

NORRIS

PICKLED

Joy of Pickling

FEARNLEY-WHITTINGSTALL

THE RIVER COTTAGE

MEAT

BOOK

TEN SPEED PRESS

SAM & SAM CLARK

MORO

SENDI

Jeffrey Alford Naomi Duguid

FLATBREADS & flavors

Morrow

FERGUS HENDERSON

THE WHOLE BEAST

Nose to Tail Eating

Jane Grigson's

English Food

Penguin

NFT

Not For Tourists Guide to San Francisco • 2005

in the sweet kitchen

REGAN DALEY

ARTISAN

ABOUT SALTIE

A Brief History of My Culinary Career and the Serendipitous Formation of Saltie

There was no romance in my formative years. I didn't seem particularly destined for a life in the food business. I never traveled to Europe, or even Montreal. I grew up in Upstate New York, just a few miles from the Culinary Institute of America— a place that absolutely no one that I knew would attend. We were all headed for college and life in some at least quasi-professional sphere. We would study uncertain curriculum like business or communications, maybe science, or, if you were willing to take the chance, the liberal arts. Mysterious and unknowable professions awaited us. There was no precedent around me for seeking a career that you could craft on your own, that you could weave of accumulated experiences. There were jobs; you chose one and carried on.

I got a degree and went to work in "the arts," as far as I could tell the most creative field on the slate. I was hired to be the production assistant in the Publications Department at the Museum of Modern Art. I figured I was set for life. A week into my esteemed position, I realized that I was just a secretary for a mean-spirited and indifferent man, whom I tried to avoid for as much of the day as possible. I stayed for the business-etiquette requisite year and then, on the day of my anniversary, handed in my notice.

I had always liked to eat. When I was growing up, my mother prepared dinner every night, according to the trends of the 1970s: pork chops cooked in orange juice, "Spanish" rice, two-hour roasted chicken, frozen vegetables, and even the occasional Jell-O salad. At least we were Italian—"one hundred percent," as my friend Dennis Spina endlessly points out. All four of my grandparents came over on the boat. We had sauce on Sundays, and later, after my parents went to Italy for the first time in 1978, a lot of pasta. Pasta with pesto, broccoli rabe, uncooked tomato sauce. When food trends changed in the '80s, we ate un-American things like ratatouille, carrots and zucchini cooked with mint, asparagus, artichokes, fresh basil, homemade pizza, and leg of lamb. It seemed like my mother, having gotten back to her Italian roots, was inspired to cook more like her mother did, forgoing an earlier notion to conform to the culinary norms of suburban life. Her cooking style changed, and I noticed.

After the museum and a series of bad jobs and happy accidents, I found myself in midtown Manhattan answering phones for a corporate caterer. Looking over at the prep kitchen, I realized that was where I wanted to be—on the other side of the order ticket. In 1993, at the age of twenty-six, I decided to go to cooking school. In what may have been an ill-considered decision at the time, I went to the Natural Gourmet Cookery School, a holistic, mostly macrobiotic cooking program on 21st Street. I didn't choose a more traditional program because I didn't want to be in a French kitchen taught by what I imagined would be yet another population of indifferent and mean men, this time perhaps with scarves knotted around their necks instead of the corporate tie. I also didn't want to spend twenty thousand dollars and two years of my life just to get a job. While I didn't know anything about the French culinary canon, I preemptively rejected its discipline—as is my tendency.

Ultimately, going to the Natural Gourmet set me on the path to independence in the culinary world. While I had no real aspiration to cook or live according to this credo, learning about macrobiotic theory and method had and continues to have a tremendous impact on how I proceed as a cook. What macrobiotics ultimately teaches are exactly the principles I learned and embraced later: how to cook and eat according to the seasons and locality; how to balance a meal; understanding the basic nutritive qualities of foods; and appreciating the power of food both to sustain and to heal. This practice instilled a reverence for food and put forth the idea that the food we take in is our responsibility: we are its stewards. I still repeat the mantra "One grain equals ten thousand grains" every time I rinse a batch of rice.

While I had only the vaguest idea of what I wanted out of a life in the kitchen, I knew with certainty what I didn't want: I didn't want to get yelled at and/or slammed every night for six hours in a two-hundred-fifty-seat restaurant working next to hyped-up boy line cooks. I wanted to avoid kitchens that were adrenaline- and testosterone-fueled endurance labs. Every fear and cliché was alive in my mind. I didn't want to be a Chef. I just wanted to learn how to cook.

Fortunately, I was spared this all-too-common scenario. My first job, at Savoy in SoHo, was a dream by industry standards: a civilized schedule in a sane and respectful house run by smart, thoughtful people who were able to teach, be firm, and inspire, all without the drama and pain associated with restaurant life. While Savoy initiated me into the physical life of cooking— I learned how to use a knife, prep with speed and efficiency, work the line—the more meaningful education was intellectual. I was introduced to the ideas that would inspire me to continue on as a cook. I learned about selection and handling of the best available fruits and vegetables; seasons and regions; and the cuisines of the world. I also learned how to break down a leg of lamb, a rack of venison, or a twenty-pound fish; debone a rabbit or a suckling pig; kill and skin an eel; cook an octopus; salt-roast a duck; stuff a sausage; and make *taramasalata, gremolata, romesco, anchoiade, fesanjan*, and *ras al hanout*.

I was hired to be the opening chef at Diner in 1998. Under different circumstances, I would never have been given a chef's job at this point in my education and experience; I had been cooking for just barely five years and hadn't worked around enough. I was solidly good, competent but not brilliant. But Diner was on the south side of Williamsburg, far from the subway and a block past the bridge. No one would ever come all that way.

It really was a diner—a salvaged 1920s Kullman dining car. A thin wood-and-metal shell over a hole in the ground. Andrew Tarlow, Mark Firth, and a stream of their friends renovated the greasy lunch counter into a glowing, jewel-like last stand. Two blocks from the water, surrounded by the building's warm dark wood, with the odd portholes above the doorways, the slatted windows . . . I always felt as if we were in the hull of a boat. With barely a foundation beneath us, it did seem that we floated.

We had no sense that we would succeed, other than maybe very modestly. We would serve our friends living across the street in the Gretsch building or on South 11th and Kent. We only needed to be good. We'd have fun. Then we'd be done.

But something unexpected happened. We were busy, far exceeding our early hopes to break even by cooking for thirty-five people a night. Andrew, Mark, Kate Huling (Andrew's then-girlfriend, now-wife), and I more or less inadvertently created a neighborhood restaurant in a neighborhood that was on the verge of redefining Brooklyn as the cultural and culinary phenomenon that we now commonly accept. Diner was a place where both the staff and the customers felt

ownership. People came for dinner, stayed late, and ended up on the bar without their pants on. There were dance parties, rock-and-roll Tuesdays, illegally built back rooms, teleportations, Gay Mondays, installations, broken glass, broken chairs, T-shirts, and tote bags. There were plenty of times when I wondered whether I worked in a restaurant or a disco. But there was also real work happening.

Within the whirlwind, a collective spirit was being created. Relationships were being forged that would change how we all felt about our work and our lives. Making hamburgers became sourcing whole animals from regional farms. Buying vegetables became a true and lasting friendship with local farmers. Creating jobs and recognizing the talents of our staff meant being able to pursue further endeavors.

The family grew. Bonita, a Mexican restaurant, was inspired by the staff meals of Jose, our best line cook. Marlow & Sons filled the space that was emptied when the exterminator next door moved across the street. Initially conceived as a market and oyster bar to complement Diner, it soon became a restaurant in its own right. The *Diner Journal* was created, a quarterly publication on food, agriculture, and art made possible by Anna Dunn, an aspiring writer and begrudging coffee maker. Another Bonita opened in Fort Greene. With a whole-animal program taking on shape and importance, Marlow & Daughters butcher shop was formed. Making dinner for thirty-five lost souls flourished into what proved to be a home, a family, a community.

Over time the food and the service got better. We all became professionals. Diner became a destination, first for those who wanted to see

what life in Williamsburg was like and then for those who wanted to see the restaurant that had changed the landscape of the neighborhood, then of the borough.

I have always been, and still am, proud to be a part of what Diner and Marlow are—to be a member of, and a collaborator in, that community. We thought that we could reinvent the system, create a different economy with our purchasing habits, our commitment to the good cause of sustainability, and by supporting our farmers and our staff. And then we would expand our sphere of influence with projects like the *Diner Journal* and the butcher shop. I went into the world every day knowing that my work and my total devotion to people and place made what I did meaningful. It was my honor.

But after eleven years, I reached the end. If another cook handed in their notice, another health inspection insulted my sensibilities, another sensitive *garde manger* who didn't want to be told he was slow stopped talking to me for the night, another new waitress asked me what my name was . . . I was tired of working nights, bored of managing the tomatoes and reorganizing the dry goods. And also, I was turning forty.

Saltie didn't start out as a concept. It began as a space: 378 Metropolitan Avenue, a bakery, formerly known as Cheeks, was up for sale. Cheeks was small, a classic five-hundred-square-foot New York City railroad apartment—the size of my apartment. But it was a sweet space, renovated and clean, with brick, tile, and tin ceilings.

During the time Cheeks was on the market, Elizabeth, Rebecca, and I found each other at the wedding of a former Diner waitress. I had just left the Diner/Marlow empire, Rebecca was out in the wilderness and unemployed

after a series of unsatisfactory kitchen jobs, and Elizabeth was working again as a pastry chef after taking a hiatus. It was Rebecca who pushed the idea of taking over Cheeks, knowing that there was nowhere left for her to work and it was time to do something else. I thought we could certainly manage this little space . . . but we still had to convince Elizabeth to quit her job. And then, what would we do with it? No room for seating, no liquor license, no bathroom. Nevertheless, despite its limitations—or maybe because of them—it just seemed right, and the three of us signed up to spend the next five years together.

Saltie is landlocked, six blocks from the East River and two blocks from the Brooklyn-Queens Expressway. Metropolitan Avenue is a truck route connecting these two boroughs, which at moments has driven me to declare that it is perhaps the loudest street in the known galaxy. We live with the daily groan of eighteen wheels downshifting toward the light; idling outside, the hydraulic brakes of the Dairyland truck; the rumble of traffic over an uninterrupted landscape of potholes; the inexplicable squeal of every single Q59 bus in the fleet passing by on an irregular schedule. And the garbage! Yet, despite the noise and general filth, Metropolitan Avenue is a corner of cozy relationships. Saltie is bound together with the City Reliquary Museum, the Commodore, Momofuku Milk Bar, the Mariella pizza guys, Metroline car service, Cupcakeland, Siam Orchid, two bodegas, and the Roebling Tea Room, all on one stretch of Metropolitan Avenue—our ragged, rugged, beloved home.

Local legend has it that the old buildings in Williamsburg were constructed from the cast-off beams used to build ships in the navy yard.

SUICIDE RISK ASSESSMENT

Prepared for: Saltie™

Major Risk Factors
1 or more women working together in close quarters
Sugar and caffeine on premises

Additional Risk Factors
Seasonal Affective Disorder
Interacting with public

1793

We could've used
a girl like you
at the Alamo

Church Mouse seeks
Good Time Charlie

HAIR PULLING
$ 1

Alert: English Breakfast Tea
sold by Porto Rico has suffered
a significant drop in quality

from Korean grocer
on Grand Street

IT WERE
ENOUGH

are in full bloom
all over the
neighborhood

Captures some of the crisp singles
and bold flavours that many of our
sea-faring explorers doubtless
enjoyed in their own time.

As we were sinking into our space, we realized that we liked to be reminded of the fact that our neighborhood, despite its trashy urban demeanor, is actually on the water. We wanted to bring the idea of the water into our space, to invoke it and the history connected to it. I wanted to connect Saltie to the thoughts I've always had about living in this peculiar confluence of water that is the island and rivers and boroughs of New York. I called upon my friend Joseph Foglia to design the space with us. We wanted it to be bright, white, and blue, with the feeling of the seaside. As we began to conceptualize what the space would be, the water came in. The materials and surfaces arrived and the space started to take on the aura of a ferry boat.

Like Saltie, the three of us are also from the water. Rebecca's dad was a shipbuilder in the seaport town of Birkenhead, in England—*and*

she's a Pisces. I grew up on the Hudson River. Elizabeth, from Minnesota, is a Saltie in reverse: she traveled from fresh water to salt. I had also spent the previous two years before we founded the shop reading *Moby Dick*, and as silly or pretentious as it may sound, finishing that book and what it left swirling around inside my head had a tremendous impact on the theme of Saltie.

With all of us, whatever endeavor we are involved in, inspiration and ideas come from all over. Restaurants are not just about food; they're about all of the forces, small and large, that have brought us to this point and place. They are who we are—our obsessions, fantasies, wishes, and quirks: *Moby Dick*; sandwiches; pastries; the beach; friends; pets; parents; neighbors; a summer in Spain or a season working at the Greenmarket; Led Zeppelin; being English, Minnesota Norwegian, or Italian American.

BRIGADE DE CUISINE

Staff, Heat, Space, and Necessary Tools

"First I need space enough to get a good simple meal for six people. More of either would be wasteful as well as dangerously dull.

Then, I need a window or two, for clear air and a sight of things growing.

Most of all I need to be let alone. I need space."
—M. F. K. FISHER

The kitchen at Saltie is a fifteen-by-eight-foot box that houses two cooks and a dishwasher named Fidel. The sandwiches, prepared by a third cook, are made in the front of the space, separated from the public by the pastry case. The counter person and the sandwich maker perform lunch service. The cooks in the back make the hot food and keep the prep going.

The heat in the kitchen at Saltie consists of the following—two Cook-Tech induction burners, which conduct heat via magnetic wave, and a convection oven with four cooking racks in it. What this basically means is we have about as much juice as anyone at home. I have come to like cooking on induction burners. They don't get slow, like gas does at most restaurants, when the burners start to clog up from use and the pilot lights burn out. They are clean, quick, and hot.

But unlike a flame, there is nothing warm or romantic about the wave-based cooking element. It's rather sterile. One way to combat this is by using "warm" cooking vessels, particularly cast iron, as well as other warm sorts of implements, like wooden spoons and a mortar and pestle. I believe, perhaps with a touch of mysticism, that the pans, bowls, spoons, and machines you use to prepare your food impart themselves into what you are making. This doesn't mean there's anything wrong with using a food processor; it just means that the food processor has an effect on the final result that should be considered going in.

This section is in essence a simple plea to be thoughtful about the tools you use. It is also here to say that you don't need much to cook well at home, but you would do well to have some basics that will make a difference.

Knives

A good knife is one that you can handle. I don't think there's an absolute knife for all. I love the design and weight of Japanese knives, as well as the ease with which they are kept sharp. At Saltie, we use the Kikuichi brand and have four carbon-steel chef's knives, four offset serrated knives, a few odd knives our neighbor was selling on the sidewalk, and many, many paring knives. Marlow & Daughters stocked Kikuichis (along with some beautiful Sabatier Nogent carbon-steel knives) when knife-obsessed Tom Mylan was the buyer for the store. As a result, everyone on staff (largely because they could buy knives at cost) jumped on the Kikuichi bandwagon. Now it seems our kitchen can't function with any one of these knives missing. (This is also true of a Swiss-style vegetable peeler.) Serrated knives are for bread and tomatoes. Paring knives for the ends of every vegetable in the kingdom.

Whether these are the knives that you too can't live without or there are others that you would put on the list, it is important to have a relationship with your knives. To this day, my mother uses a flimsy, plastic-handled serrated supermarket steak knife to prepare everything she cooks. She can make dinner for twenty with this one excruciatingly little knife. I can't even bear to use it to pry open a can, but she would be lost without it. And I understand. Regardless of the knife you choose, it is important only that it be a knife that you believe in.

Spoons

At Saltie, we talk about spoons a lot. There are particular spoons for particular jobs. We each have our favorites and the ones we shun, unable to understand how anyone could ever use them. There are some that we fight over and others that we wonder who bought them or why. I cook only with wooden spoons; I can't stand the interaction of a metal spoon in a pot or pan. Metal spoons are used for mixing things in bowls and for plating sandwich ingredients and salads.

Mortar and Pestle

In this book, the classic, but somewhat forsaken, duo of mortar and pestle will get mentioned again and again. I think it's particularly handy to use a mortar and pestle at home when you just need a little of something. I use it for pounding garlic, grinding spices, and (most often) to refine the very coarse gray sea salt that I prefer. A mortar and pestle set is one of those things that you can live without until you have one.

Cast Iron

"If you are one of those who feel that some special virtue attaches to a venerable black iron pan unwashed for twenty years, then you are probably right to cling to it."
—ELIZABETH DAVID

For the purposes of this book, a cast-iron skillet and Dutch oven are essential, especially for making potato tortilla and naan. I find cast iron to be preferable to other pots and pans for preparing just about anything. Food doesn't stick in well-seasoned cast iron. It is a soft metal and behaves much more smoothly and reliably than other materials. Cast iron also conducts heat evenly and, perhaps most important, develops a personality. Really, it does.

Egg Pans

We cook a lot of eggs at Saltie, and therefore we reluctantly use Teflon nonstick pans. The only reason we use these pans is the Cook-Tech burner requires that the pan have a reactive alloy in its base. We haven't found a pan that works better given this condition.

At home I use a Calphalon nonstick pan that my mother bought for me. I'm not exactly sure what Calphalon is, but I like these pans more than I am comfortable admitting. They are highly reactive and much smoother than stainless steel, which is really hard—literally—to cook with, and I don't like using for much at all. Carbon-steel sauté pans are also great for egg cookery. Much like cast iron, these pans become seasoned and will develop their own nonstick qualities over time.

While "soft," "warm," and "hard" may not be strictly technical terms for why pots and pans produce (or don't) certain results, they describe the essence of the metal, regarding its impact on the cooking process and the character of the final dish. The more you cook, the more you will choose certain implements and vessels over others and you will start to form your own opinions about what you like.

Miscellany

We also rely heavily on a food processor and a blender; produce from Guy Jones and Lancaster Farm Fresh; regular mental-health evaluations, humor-based visits, and postcards from Walter Sipser; financial advice from Kirsten Fazzari; medical advice from Kristin Gaughn; morning visits and afternoon snacks from Stephen Tanner and Luke Roberts; a regular check-in from Dennis Spina; beer and comic relief from Millicent Souris; the devoted support of Chloe Schwartz, Juliet Dostalek, and Andrea Mersits for keeping it together; Jill Meerpohl and Fidel for maintaining our standards; spiritual advice from Planet Waves; the guidance of our great teachers; four iPods; and a steady stream of friends and neighbors. Armed with the material and transcendent necessities, our *brigade de cuisine* moves forth.

NOTES ON
KEY INGREDIENTS

Brightness, Salt, and Flavor

In most cases, the addition of olive oil and salt, and often lemon, will make anything taste better. Cooking well, beyond basic technique, is developing the ability to properly season a dish. Most failures in the kitchen tend to suffer less from being cooked poorly than from a lack of brightness or salt—essentially the loss of the quality of being, or once having been, alive. Luckily, this is a particularly easy problem to remedy. First, buy the best raw materials—your fruits, vegetables, and proteins ideally should be well sourced, seasonal, and local whenever possible. Beyond that, simply stocking lemons, good sea salt, and olive oil will make almost anything a pleasure to eat. Grains, beans, and greens truly require nothing more than these three ingredients.

Salt

In the beginning, the only salt I thought about was kosher. The thrill of kosher salt so nicely coarse that you could grab it with your fingers was enough for me. At that time, I was unaware of the very existence of sea salt, let alone its remarkable qualities. The main difference between good sea salt and kosher salt is that sea salt tastes like something beyond salty—not to mention that it is naturally harvested, unprocessed, and contains a balanced mineral content. Like so many other things, once you get used to it, it's hard to go back. I like to use coarse gray sea salt from France. It tastes minerally, it is salty in a savory way, and the large grains add crunch and texture. It's worth picking up a bag of sea salt. There's nothing better for finishing a dish, to sprinkle over salad, fresh ricotta, or a ripe tomato.

I still use kosher salt at work for big brawny salting, for seasoning water for cooking pasta or potatoes, or for salting stews and soups.

Black Pepper

For a long time, I automatically salted and peppered everything I was cooking. I didn't think about it; I just did it. Animal, vegetable, fish, I seasoned them all in the same way. I realize now that I was absentminded, not thinking about the quality of this particular seasoning and how it might impose itself on a preparation. These days the only thing I pepper as part of the cooking process is meat. Otherwise I use pepper exclusively as a finishing agent, when the dish calls for a cracking of fresh black pepper. For this, I use the pepper mill, with consideration for whether it will improve the dish or not. I think that black pepper should always be used in this considered way.

Olive Oil

Like salt, there is olive oil you cook with and olive oil you finish with. I always keep three types of olive oil in the kitchen: a commercial-use extra-virgin olive oil (fancyish and cold pressed), "pure" olive oil (a workaday blended but still all-olive oil), and finishing oil (comparatively expensive artisan extra-virgin oils that are richer and more nuanced).

Contrary to the prevailing kitchen wisdom that heating extra-virgin oil isn't worth the price or even will impart an "off" quality, I cook everything in extra-virgin olive oil. I find that everything tastes better cooked in this medium. That said, we are never really cooking anything at such a high heat that its lower smoke point is a concern; I think that for most home cooking this is true as well.

We use pure olive oil only for making mayonnaise. With the exception of mayonnaise and aioli, when the words "olive oil" are used in a recipe in this book, they mean extra-virgin.

Finally, we use the finishing oils on hand for drizzling over prepared food or salads. For this I like to try different oils and will choose one using a criteria similar to how I would choose a bottle of wine—perhaps one that I recognize and that is in the range of what I am prepared to spend, including one that seems worth a little extra.

Lemons

Always have a good supply of lemons. Lemons are often all you need to elevate a dish from bland to alive. Developing a sense about when a dish needs acid is crucial to your success and one of the most essential things to know in the kitchen.

Garlic (and a Small Rant on Purchasing Habits)

If you live in New York, most of the garlic for sale in supermarkets, bodegas, or Korean delis is from China. I have come to view these cloves as completely sinister. Not because of an ethical concern, but because here, contained in this head of garlic, is a glaring example of how completely out of order our food system is and how important it is to know what you are buying and eating. It's cheaper to buy garlic grown across the world than it is to buy it from a farmer less than one hundred miles from home. Garlic from China is more commodity than foodstuff. It is produced for a global market, shipped unreasonable distances, and still maintains a lower price point than anything that can be grown domestically. While we may enjoy cheap garlic, when we choose these things, we imperil our local food system. In the end, all that we are left with is cheapened food produced by whatever means necessary to keep it cheap.

Witness the evolution of local garlic over the course of a season and understand the difference between what is real and what is just stuff produced for a market of endless demand. Local food economies protect us from losing one of our most valuable entitlements—choice over what we eat and transparency about how it was produced. Buy your garlic from a local farm whenever possible; otherwise look for garlic from California.

CHAPTER 1

BASICS

"I never really wanted to be involved in food. It's something that I'm good at and I obviously enjoy. I started out as a dishwasher and thought cooking would be easier than washing dishes. It's not that I wanted to be a chef. I don't think anybody, if they saw the amount of work and how crappy it is, would want that." —RC

I learned how to think about food and write menus by reading cookbooks and eating out. I have stolen many recipes and ideas and made them my own. The very question of what makes an "original" recipe original is continually disputed, and there may very well be recipes in this book that came from somewhere else but that I have used for so long I can't remember what the original source is. Some chefs are blessed with creative genius, and some of us are good cooks who know how to make what we know how to make. Recipes go around and around, and when you begin to understand the culinary language and landscape, you find yourself making new dishes that are actually very old—inventing things that already exist. Once you become fully engaged in the art of cooking, in its history and traditions, you will discover the collective culinary unconscious, the wisdom of the ages.

Over years of cooking you start to notice your tendencies—certain recipes or ingredients that you rely on. This may kindly be called "style," but in less creative moments one can be nagged by a feeling that it's merely repetition. You find yourself saying the same things over and over, like "It needs a little acid," or "This could use an herb." I've come to realize that the phenomenon does not mean I am incapable of coming up with anything new; it is simply the proof of one of many truths: Everything tastes better with a squeeze of lemon and a handful of parsley.

These affinities start to accumulate and become the underlying foundation that gives structure to what you do—the qualities that make your food unique to you. Every good restaurant has its own set of basics. These elements don't have to be original—they can be stolen; co-opted or adapted; classical or contemporary. They are the building blocks of flavor—simple recipes or combinations of ingredients that are called upon again and again to make a dish rise to the standard.

At Saltie, we make big, over-the-top sandwiches that are fresh, bold, and appealing—some say addictive. We use classical recipes and techniques that have been around for hundreds of years. Our basics are focaccia and naan; mayonnaises and vinaigrettes; classic sauces; herby mixes; yogurt and yogurt sauce; eggs cooked in various ways; and pickles. We didn't invent any of these, but we know their powers and how to use them well.

Breads

Perhaps one of the things that distinguishes the sandwiches at Saltie is the idea that they are not just sandwiches but in fact complete little meals on bread. Culinary microcosms. Staged experiences. Dioramas. When we developed them, we did it in the same way that we would a restaurant menu. Bread is just the delivery system. In our minds we weren't opening a sandwich shop per se, but a little shop where we could serve the things we like to make and eat. The only real difference conceptually between this food and the food we've made anywhere else is the presence or absence of bread.

Take away the bread and the Captain's Daughter makes a perfect appetizer of sardines, pickled eggs, and *salsa verde*. The Scuttlebutt is a Greek salad. The Spanish Armada is lunch or a snack with a glass of rosé. The Clean Slate is a mezze plate.

And although I may have just portrayed bread as expendable, we knew that the vehicle had to be equally as considered and distinctive as that which it transports. We knew immediately that we could not make sandwiches without making our own bread. We also wanted to get away from what have become standard sandwich breads like baguette or Pullman loaves. The bread we would choose would need to work well with anything that may come to rest between it. It needed to be special, adaptable and simple to produce. We settled on focaccia and naan.

Focaccia

Focaccia is the bread that we use for most of the sandwiches at Saltie. The reasons for choosing this soft-but-chewy Italian yeast bread were equally pragmatic and delicious. We considered what we could reasonably produce and decided a bread that we could make on a baking sheet would be much more economical in terms of time and space than one that required more individual attention. As has been the case with many of our choices at Saltie, landing on focaccia at first may have seemed the solution to how to do something in the best and most efficient way, but it quickly became the fact-of-the-matter only possible choice that it is today. Now I can't imagine life without focaccia. Its fluffy, oily welcome greets me daily.

6¼ cups all-purpose flour

2 tablespoons kosher salt

1 teaspoon active dry yeast

3½ cups warm water

¼ cup extra-virgin olive oil, plus more for greasing and drizzling

Coarse sea salt

ENOUGH FOR 8-10 SANDWICHES

In a large bowl, whisk together the flour, salt, and yeast. Add the warm water to the flour mixture and stir with a wooden spoon until all the flour is incorporated and a sticky dough forms (no kneading required). Pour the ¼ cup olive oil into a 6-quart plastic food container with a tight-fitting lid (see Note). Transfer the focaccia dough to the plastic container, turn to coat, and cover tightly. Place in the refrigerator to rise for at least 8 hours or for up to 2 days.

When you're ready to bake, oil an 18-by-13-inch baking sheet. Remove the focaccia dough from the refrigerator and transfer to the prepared pan. Using your hands, spread the dough out on the prepared pan as much as possible, adding oil to the dough as needed to keep it from sticking. Place the dough in a warm place and let rise until about doubled in bulk. The rising time will vary considerably depending on the season. (In the summer, it may take only 20 minutes for the dough to warm up and rise; in the winter it can take an hour or more.) When the dough is ready, it should be room temperature, spread out on the sheet, and fluffy feeling.

Preheat the oven to 450°F.

CONTINUED

Pat down the focaccia to an even thickness of about 1 inch on the baking sheet tray and begin to make indentations in the dough with your fingertips. Dimple the entire dough and then drizzle the whole thing again with olive oil. Sprinkle the entire surface of the focaccia evenly with sea salt.

Bake, rotating once front to back, until the top is uniformly golden brown, about 15 minutes. Transfer to a wire rack to cool, then slide out of the pan. Use the same day.

NOTE: This easy recipe calls for a large plastic food-storage container, about a 6-quart capacity, with a tight-fitting lid. Otherwise, you can use a large mixing bowl and cover the dough with plastic wrap.

Unfortunately, focaccia suffers a rapid and significant deterioration in quality after the first day. It is also impossible to make bread crumbs with focaccia. Ideally, bake and eat focaccia on the same day. If there is some left over, wrap it tightly in plastic and store at room temperature for one day more. Day-old focaccia is delicious in soup.

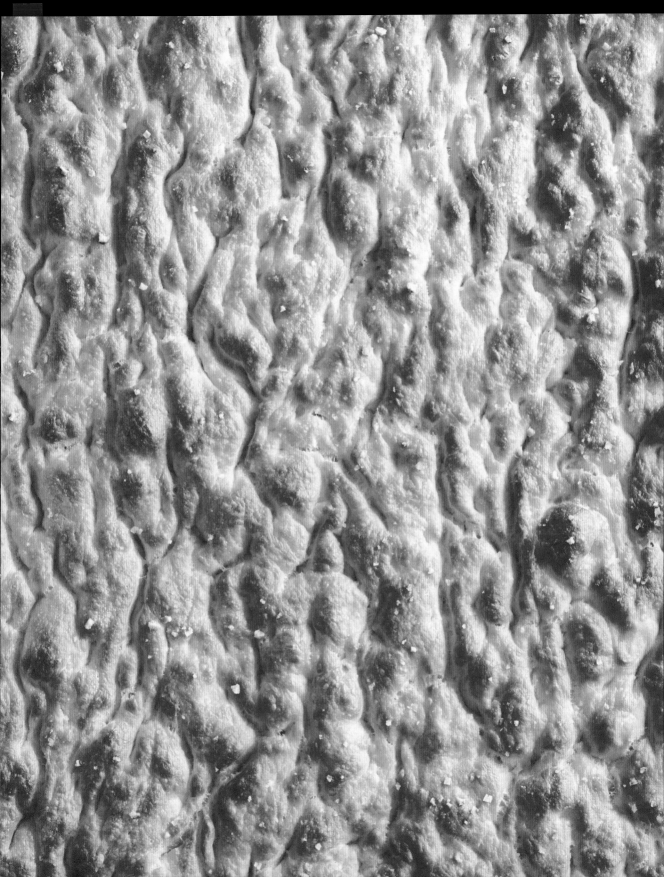

Naan

2 cups all-purpose flour,
plus more for dusting

¾ cup whole-grain spelt flour

1 teaspoon kosher salt

½ teaspoon baking powder

1⅓ cups buttermilk or yogurt

Extra-virgin olive oil for frying

Whenever I am cooking this naan in a cast-iron skillet, the smell of it drives me crazy and I have to fight the urge to eat one right then and there. Far from exotic or complicated, naan is so fantastic and easy it seems a shame to me that chances are most people, even avid cooks, will never try. But please do try! Making naan is not like making bread. It's quick, easy, and fun. You can mix it by hand, and it's ready in a flash. It smells great, tastes great, and is a wonderful complement to just about anything.

In a large bowl, whisk together both flours, the salt, and baking powder. Add the buttermilk and stir it into the flour with a wooden spoon. When the dough becomes too stiff to mix with a spoon, dust your hands with flour and knead the dough in the bowl until the dry and wet ingredients are thoroughly incorporated. Cover the bowl with plastic wrap or store in a plastic container with a tight-fitting lid. Refrigerate the dough for at least 1 hour or up to 2 days.

When you're ready to cook, remove the dough from the refrigerator, dust your work surface liberally with flour, and portion the naan dough into 3½- to 4-ounce balls (use a scale, or alternatively, make balls that are roughly 3½ inches in diameter). This dough will be very sticky—don't be afraid to use a lot of flour to handle it. Roll out each ball of dough into a circle about 7 inches in diameter.

Heat a dry cast-iron skillet over high heat until smoking. Drizzle 1 tablespoon olive oil around the skillet. Pick up a naan circle, stretch it out a bit more all around, shake off any excess flour, and place it in the skillet. When the naan starts to bubble, after about 1 minute, drizzle another 1 tablespoon of olive oil over the surface and use tongs or a metal spatula to flip it. The first side should be deep brown, even charred. Cook until there is no visible raw flour and the surface is speckled brown, 1 to 2 minutes longer. Transfer to a plate and keep warm in a low oven while you fry the rest of the naan.

Serve warm. Wrap any leftover naan in plastic wrap for up to 2 days. Reheat in a 350°F oven until warm.

Spreads, Dressings, and Sauces

Mayonnaise, vinaigrette, herb mixes, purées, and pickles are the sort of refrigerated pantry items that we keep in stock and use as the foundation for most of what we make at Saltie. If there is a question of what something needs or out of what to make a special, a trip to the condiments department often makes the decision for us. Often we will make things like pesto or herb sauces, *romesco*, or hot sauce to have on hand that will later become part of an egg bowl or be used to garnish a soup. While most of these items don't have an indefinite shelf life, they will hold up well for a week or two so that we are not always scrambling to come up with something new.

A sandwich requires a dressing. A dressing can be mayonnaise, mustard, oil, vinegar, or butter. It is what drives the sandwich, makes it palatable, loosens it up. Mayonnaise is the most luxurious of dressings. To make mayonnaise is to make one of the great emulsion-based sauces in the culinary canon. Mayonnaise has a long and esteemed history and should be held in proper praise as one of gastronomy's great gifts. The fact that mayonnaise has become equated with a quick and unhealthful indulgence scooped out of a plastic tub is a tragedy. Make it yourself and see it redeemed.

This recipe is for mayonnaise (pictured on page 46 in the red bowl) made in a food processor. You can certainly make mayonnaise by hand with a whisk and a bowl. I encourage you to try that at least once, especially when making a small batch; it's a great hands-on exhibit of the chemistry of emulsifying and it's very satisfying to make happen. If making mayonnaise by hand, you may not need to add the water, because you will not be able to whisk at the speed of the food processor and your mayonnaise will not thicken up as quickly.

Mayonnaise

2 egg yolks

1 teaspoon white wine vinegar

1 teaspoon Dijon mustard

1½ teaspoons kosher salt,
plus more for seasoning

2 cups pure olive oil (see Note)

4 tablespoons water,
or as needed

Juice of ½ lemon (optional)

MAKES ABOUT 2 CUPS

Combine the egg yolks, vinegar, mustard, and 1½ teaspoons salt in a food processor and pulse to mix. With the machine running, begin to add the olive oil in a slow, steady stream. After adding about one-third of the oil, the mixture will start to come together. You will be able to hear this as well as see it. Initially you will hear the whoosh of the ingredients in the machine deepen, and then it will quiet as the mayonnaise starts to thicken. At this point add 2 tablespoons of the water to thin the mayonnaise and prevent it from breaking.

Continue to add the oil. As the mixture thickens up again, add the remaining 2 tablespoons water, a little at a time, just as needed to correct the consistency. Once all of the oil has been added, turn off the machine and taste the mayonnaise. Add more salt as necessary. Also taste for acidity; if the mayonnaise seems a little flat, add the lemon juice to brighten it.

The mayonnaise will keep, covered tightly in the refrigerator, for up to 1 week.

NOTE: I don't like to use extra-virgin olive oil in either mayonnaise or aioli. I find it to be too strong and rather bitter. Many recipes, especially for aioli, will call for extra-virgin for at least for a portion of the oil used. Experiment and decide what you like, but be aware that the final product will be different from the one that we are suggesting.

VARIATION: CURRIED MAYONNAISE (pictured on page 46 in the blue bowl) Follow the main recipe, adding 1 tablespoon curry powder to the food processor with the egg yolks in the first step.

We make this aioli (pictured on the facing page in the yellow bowl) at Saltie with garlic and *pimentón*, a smoked paprika from Spain that is a particular favorite of Rebecca's—it's like her magic powder. *Pimentón* is one of those things that seems like a cheat, because it comes out of a cute little tin yet imparts a depth of flavor that is hard to put your finger on. Smoky? Yes, but bright and aromatic, easy and balanced. It seems to make everything taste better.

Aioli is simply garlic mayonnaise and can be variously seasoned with herbs, citrus, or spices. It can also be used without any flavor other than the assertive garlic.

Pimentón Aioli

2 large garlic cloves

1 teaspoon sea salt

2 egg yolks

1½ teaspoons *pimentón*

1 tablespoon plus 1 teaspoon sherry vinegar

2 cups pure olive oil

4 tablespoons water, or as needed

Kosher salt

MAKES ABOUT 2 CUPS

Put the garlic in a mortar with the sea salt and pound into a paste with a pestle. The sea salt will act as an abrasive and assist in breaking down the garlic. If you don't have a mortar and pestle, mince the garlic on a cutting board, sprinkle with the sea salt, and continue to mince until the salt is well incorporated and starts to break down the garlic. Make a paste by spreading the mixture on the board with the flat side of your knife blade. Continue along, alternating between chopping and spreading until you have achieved a smooth paste.

Transfer the garlic paste to a food processor. Add the egg yolks, *pimentón*, and vinegar and pulse to mix. With the machine running, begin to add the olive oil in a slow, steady stream. After adding about one-third of the oil, the mixture will start to come together. Add 2 tablespoons of the water to thin the aioli and prevent it from breaking.

Continue to add the oil. As the mixture thickens up again, add the remaining 2 tablespoons water, a little at a time, just as needed to correct the consistency. Once all of the oil has been added, turn off the machine and taste the aioli. If additional seasoning is needed, add a pinch of kosher salt, which will dissolve more easily at this point.

The aioli will keep, covered tightly in the refrigerator, for up to 1 week.

We call this versatile dressing "Lazy Housewife" because you just have to shake it up in a jar and it's ready to go. It is a basic mustard vinaigrette that you can make quickly without having to worry about whisking and emulsifying. It's great on leafy salads, grain-based salads, or bean salads. Make a big batch and store it in the refrigerator. It will hold well for up to 1 week. After that, the garlic or shallot is liable to get funny.

Lazy Housewife Vinaigrette

2 large garlic cloves, thinly sliced, or 1 shallot, thinly sliced

2 teaspoons Dijon mustard

1 teaspoon minced fresh thyme (optional)

A generous pinch of sea salt

½ cup red wine vinegar

1½ cups extra-virgin olive oil

Put the garlic, mustard, thyme (if using), sea salt, and vinegar in a mason jar or any container with a screw-on top. Screw the top on tightly and shake to mix well. Uncover and add the olive oil. Close tightly again and shake until well mixed. The vinaigrette will keep, tightly covered in the refrigerator, for 1 week.

NOTE: This is a basic framework, the details of which can be altered to taste. While the recommended vinegar for this recipe is red wine, you can certainly substitute sherry vinegar, white wine, apple cider, etc. The herb note can also be changed; rosemary, sage, savory, or tarragon will each work and lend something different, so try substituting those, depending on the qualities you are looking for. You can also use Pommery, whole-grain mustard, or a mix of the two in place of the Dijon.

Guy Jones and Lancaster Farm Fresh Cooperative, our two main sources for produce, both have plenty of fresh nettles to offer come spring. In both cases, I know it's because these guys are smart—they go out and forage before anything cultivated is ready. Guy refers to this wild produce as "God's stuff." And bless him for selling it to do-gooders like me who'll buy anything he offers. Nettles are not gleefully coveted, like their seasonal colleague and superstar the ramp, but they are solid and entirely of themselves. It seems that nettles arrive and never go away, waiting for someone to finally break down and make something of them. Embrace them (with your heart, not your hands) and discover their well-concealed charms.

Don't touch the nettles with your bare hands; they really do sting. Wear kitchen gloves to handle them.

Nettle Sauce

Kosher salt

1 large bunch stinging nettles

2 garlic cloves

Sea salt

Extra-virgin olive oil or water

Freshly ground black pepper

Juice of 1 lemon

Bring a stockpot of water generously salted with kosher salt to a boil. Have ready a large bowl of ice water.

While the water is heating, wearing kitchen gloves, pick the nettle leaves from the stalks.

When the water has come to a boil, put the garlic into the pot and blanch for 1 minute. Remove the garlic and put aside. Add the nettle leaves to the boiling water and blanch just until the water comes back up to a boil. Using a slotted spoon or tongs, lift the nettles from the stockpot and shock in the ice bath. Drain thoroughly and then squeeze out any additional water. (The nettles are now safe to handle without gloves.)

Place the garlic and nettles into the bowl of a food processor. Add a good pinch of sea salt and process to a purée. Thin with olive oil and/or water as needed to make the sauce well blended and loose. Season with sea salt, pepper, and lemon juice.

Store in a container with a tight-fitting lid in the refrigerator for up to 3 days.

Pesto and *pistou*: two classic basil sauces, one Italian, one French. The difference between them is that Italian pesto includes nuts and cheese and French *pistou* is a simpler, greener herb sauce. I find them to be equally useful and different enough to warrant including both here. One always shows itself to be more appropriate than the other depending on what I am making. Pesto has certainly been well represented in the United States in the last few decades and even abused in our American adaptation of it. At Saltie, we use pesto when we have some mozzarella or tomatoes in the house. *Pistou*, less maligned, would classically be added to a spring or summer soup before serving. We use it as a good all-around herby sauce, drizzled on vegetables or tossed with beans or grains.

For either, you can use different herbs in place of the commonly conjured basil. In fact, both are great ways to use and understand other herbs and greens.

Pesto and Pistou

8 garlic cloves

½ cup pine nuts

Sea salt

Leaves of 1 large bunch fresh basil

¼ cup extra-virgin olive oil

1 cup grated Parmigiano-Reggiano or *pecorino toscano*

Freshly ground black pepper

PESTO

Put the garlic, pine nuts, and a pinch of salt in a food processor, blender, or mortar and process or pound with a pestle to a coarse purée. Add the basil leaves and drizzle in the olive oil to loosen the mixture as you continue to process or pound. Mix until the pesto is well blended but not perfectly smooth. Transfer to a clean bowl, stir in the cheese, and season with pepper and additional salt, if needed.

The pesto can also be made with a chef's knife on a cutting board—just chop the garlic and pine nuts together finely and fairly uniformly and then start incorporating the basil and olive oil, a little at a time. It will be a bit rougher but just fine.

Cover with plastic wrap, pressing it against the surface of the pesto, and refrigerate for up to 3 days.

Leaves of 1 large bunch fresh basil

4 to 6 garlic cloves

Sea salt

¼ to ½ cup extra-virgin olive oil

Freshly ground black pepper

Juice of 1 lemon

PISTOU

In a food processor, blender, or mortar, combine the basil, garlic to taste, and a good pinch of sea salt. Process or pound with a pestle to a coarse purée. As you work, slowly drizzle in just enough olive oil to make the *pistou* well blended and loose. Season with salt, pepper, and lemon juice.

Cover with plastic wrap, pressing it against the surface of the *pistou*, and refrigerate for up to 3 days.

Romesco

4 ancho chiles

4 pasilla chiles

4 New Mexico chiles

½ cup blanched almonds
(see Note)

½ cup blanched hazelnuts
(see Note)

One 28-ounce can whole
plum tomatoes

Extra-virgin olive oil

Kosher salt

2 medium Spanish onions,
cut into chunks

12 garlic cloves, peeled but
left whole

One 5-inch square of Focaccia
(page 36), cut into cubes

2 teaspoons *pimentón*

MAKES ABOUT 4 CUPS

Romesco is a Catalan sauce. I first learned about this sauce when I worked at Savoy. Peter Hoffman annually celebrates the arrival of the spring onion as they do in Spain, with a party where the green onions are grilled and served with generous bowls of *romesco* and plenty of rosé.

We find ourselves sometimes eating this sauce by the spoonful. The combination of the nuts and chiles makes *romesco* wholly satisfying. While this is a Spanish sauce, most of the dried chiles readily available to us in the United States are Mexican varieties. I like to use a combination of chiles and choose those that are milder and not too smoky. However, experimenting with other varieties is completely appropriate. It would also be fine to use just one type of chile; for this recipe, an ancho or New Mexico variety would do well.

This is a long recipe and may seem overwhelming. Don't be discouraged. While it may involve many steps, there is nothing complicated about this procedure. Keep in mind that you are really just toasting and puréeing everything.

Heat a cast-iron skillet over medium-high heat. When the pan is hot, working in batches, put the chiles in the dry pan and toast, turning them once, until they puff up and char a little, about 2 minutes per batch. Using tongs, transfer each chile as it's finished to a plate. When all of the chiles are toasted and are cool enough to handle, pull the stem end from each. Shake out the seeds and discard.

Put the toasted and seeded chiles in a small saucepan and add water to cover. Bring to a boil over high heat, then immediately remove from the heat and let the chiles cool in the water.

Position a rack in the upper part of the oven and another rack in the middle and preheat to 400°F. Spread the almonds and hazelnuts in a single layer on a baking sheet and toast in the center of the oven until fragrant and lightly browned, about 5 minutes. Set aside and let cool. Leave the oven on.

Drain the tomatoes and arrange on a baking sheet. Drizzle with olive oil and sprinkle with salt. Slide onto the upper rack of the oven and roast until a little charred, about 20 minutes. At the same time, on a second baking sheet, toss the onions with a drizzling of olive oil and a few pinches of salt. Place on the middle rack of the oven and roast, stirring once or twice, until charred, 20 to 30 minutes.

Meanwhile, put the garlic in a small saucepan over medium-low heat and add enough olive oil just to cover. Bring to a gentle simmer and cook until the garlic turns golden, about 5 minutes. Using a slotted spoon, transfer the garlic to a bowl. Add the bread cubes to the hot oil and fry, using a wooden spoon to turn as needed, until golden on all sides, about 5 minutes total. Transfer to the bowl with the garlic and let cool. Reserve the oil.

Combine the garlic, focaccia, almonds, and hazelnuts in a food processor and process to a coarse purée. Drain the chiles, reserving the cooking water. Add the chiles and onions to the food processor and continue to purée. Finally, add the tomatoes and *pimentón*. Pulse to mix well, adding a little of the reserved chile water as needed to keep the machine moving. You want a thick, rough purée. Transfer to a serving bowl. Taste and adjust the seasoning with salt and the reserved olive oil. Serve right away, or transfer to a container with a tight-fitting lid and refrigerate. The *romesco* will keep well for up to 2 weeks. Bring to room temperature before serving.

NOTE: If you can't find blanched almonds or hazelnuts, it's really fine to use them with the skin on. For the hazelnuts, it is reasonably easy to remove the skins by toasting them in a 350°F oven until golden under the skins, about 7 minutes, then rubbing in a clean kitchen towel to loosen the skins.

While it's easy enough these days to find great yogurt produced by good farms, when you are using it in quantity, it may still prove to be either unavailable or prohibitively expensive. There is also the issue of the plastic container—I can no longer bring myself to buy yogurt in a plastic quart container, or worse, an individual serving. But we don't make our own yogurt just for reasons of economy or environmental conscience. It's exciting to make yogurt. The simple process of turning milk into yogurt overnight is a thrill.

In order to make yogurt, you need to invite bacterial culture into milk. To activate this process, you will need to have some yogurt as a starter. From then on, you can use your stock of yogurt to start the next batch.

Homemade Yogurt

1 quart whole milk, preferably fresh and organic

1 tablespoon best-quality yogurt

In a saucepan, heat the milk over medium-high heat, uncovered, until scalding but not boiling, or until an instant-read thermometer registers 180°F. Remove from the heat and let the milk cool to 110°F, about 30 minutes.

(For those without a kitchen thermometer—you don't need one. The 180°F mark is right before the milk is about come to a boil. You can pretty much see it—tiny bubbles begin to form around the edges of the pan. And 110°F is when you can put your [clean] finger in the milk and the milk is still nice and warm but comfortable enough to leave your finger in.)

Add the yogurt to the warm milk, but don't stir it. Pour the milk into a glass or plastic container with a tight-fitting lid and leave the mixture at room temperature for at least 8 hours or up to 12 hours. Once the container is set down for the night, don't agitate it or its contents. Refrigerate in the morning, once the yogurt has set up (it will look like yogurt, not milk). Homemade yogurt has about the same shelf life as store-bought.

We tend to put yogurt sauce on everything that doesn't have mayonnaise on it. We want our yogurt to be made with good milk that we choose, and we like to make everything in-house, so we make our own yogurt. We recommend you do, too; but if you don't prefer, or have time, to make your own, we understand.

Yogurt Sauce

1 pint whole-milk plain yogurt, homemade (see facing page), or good-quality store-bought

6 scallions, thinly sliced

¼ cup chopped fresh dill

3 tablespoons extra-virgin olive oil

Sea salt

White wine vinegar

MAKES 1 PINT

In a large bowl, whisk together the yogurt, scallions, and dill. Whisk in the olive oil, then season with salt and a splash of vinegar. This sauce should taste savory, with the tanginess of the yogurt mellowed.

Serve right away, or transfer the yogurt sauce to a container with a tight-fitting lid and store in the refrigerator for up to 3 days.

NOTE: There are many other seasonings you can use with this yogurt sauce. In winter we use dried sumac in place of a fresh herb. Variations include the addition of garlic, shallots, mint, and cucumbers.

Salsa verde literally means "green sauce." This is the Italian version, not the Mexican. The Mexican condiment is the *salsa verde* we are all probably more accustomed to, a spicy sauce of tomatillo, fresh chile pepper, and cilantro. While we also make plenty of Mexican style *salsa verde*, we find the following herby recipe to be versatile and indispensible, a good, all-around stand-alone mix of herbs and capers. We find this sauce to be almost salad-like, especially complementary to fish and fatty meats or simply spooned onto bread.

Salsa Verde

2 cups Fresh Herb Mix
(page 58)

¼ cup capers

1 fresh red chile (optional),
seeded and thinly sliced

2 large garlic cloves (optional),
thinly sliced

3 tablespoons extra-virgin
olive oil

Juice of 1 to 2 lemons

Sea salt

In a bowl, toss the herbs with the capers, chile and garlic (if using), and olive oil. Add the juice of 1 lemon and a small pinch of sea salt. Taste. The flavor should be bright and lemony. Adjust as necessary with lemon and salt. Serve and eat immediately. (The *salsa verde* will wilt and break down as it sits.)

Herb Butter

1 cup (2 sticks) unsalted butter, softened

2 shallots, minced

¼ cup minced fresh parsley

1 tablespoon minced fresh chives

1 tablespoon finely grated lemon zest

½ teaspoon sea salt

We use this herb butter for The Gam (page 117), a sandwich modeled after the French baguette with butter and ham. This recipe is useful for all kinds of preparations. You can serve it with fish; chicken; roasted, steamed, or sautéed vegetables; or on toast.

Put the butter in a bowl and mash with a fork. Add the remaining ingredients and mix with a fork or your fingers until everything is evenly distributed. Put into a container with a tight-fitting lid and refrigerate. Herb butter will keep for up to 1 week in the refrigerator or up to 1 month in the freezer.

We use a lot of herbs. In the early days, when it was just the three of us, picking the leaves of an herb from its sprig was a big part of our setup. It seemed we were always running out of them. Each morning Elizabeth would do the baking, I would make the potato tortilla and the drinks, and Rebecca would prep the aioli, the herb mix, and the radishes. We were so fixed in our routines that it got to the point where Rebecca didn't want anyone else to handle the herbs at all—"No, no, I'll do them." The herb mix is tedious and slow going, no way around it, and on those days when the parsley leaves are really teeny, it can be excruciating. I don't really have the patience for prepping herbs on a fixed schedule or under duress; it makes me uptight. I like to prepare them in a more

Fresh Herb Mix

1 bunch fresh parsley

1 bunch fresh mint

1 bunch fresh dill

1 small bunch fresh cilantro (optional)

1 bunch scallions, white and tender green parts, thinly sliced on the diagonal

leisurely manner. But Rebecca stood there each morning, in front of the lowboy, chewing a sprig of chive, listening to Arthur Russell, fortifying herself for the day ahead.

Herbs, probably more than anything else—maybe a lemon would compete—are key to brightness and freshness. These qualities cannot be underestimated. The addition of a fresh herb to any dish not only is welcome, but can actually make all the difference.

Here is our go-to house mix of herbs. Use it in green salads, grains, beans, soups, or to make *salsa verde*. The cilantro is optional for two reasons: a lot of people don't like it, which I am trying to be big about, and sometimes cilantro doesn't quite go with a particular preparation. This may also occasionally be true of dill or mint.

Pick the leaves from all the herb sprigs. Rinse and dry thoroughly. If the dill is very large and feathery, cut it down a little, but otherwise keep the leaves whole, or at least no more torn than what happened when you removed them from the stems.

Combine all the herbs in a bowl along with the scallions and toss to mix well. Store in a plastic container in the refrigerator for up to 2 days.

Eggs

Eggs are an essential element of any culinary repertoire. Eggs can elevate a salad or a side dish to a proper lunch or dinner and, when purchased from a local, sustainable source, are an inexpensive way to add protein, richness, and substance to a meal. Much like mayonnaise, eggs get a bad rap. When well sourced and prepared, both are nutritious, fortifying, and unfairly accused of posing a heart-health concern. This is conditional, based on the egg you choose. We buy only eggs that are pasture raised by reliable farmers. It's much easier to champion the virtues of an egg that has been properly procured.

The following recipes are for the basic egg preparations we use daily at Saltie: scrambled, sunny, boiled, and pickled. Although we would never make a poached egg at the shop—no space to devote to a simmering pot of water all day, plus I have a phobia about poached eggs (even though I've made hundreds of them)—I certainly encourage anyone who would like to substitute a poached egg over those we recommend to do so. We also occasionally recommend a poached egg, as we have in the recipe for Succotash on page 148.

The essential goal for scrambling an egg is to leave it soft. There is nothing more depressing than a dry, brown scramble of eggs—you lose all the beauty and joy. I use Rebecca's method here. She claims this is a Spanish technique, and I like the sound of that. Ideally the soft-scrambled egg (pictured on page 65, top) runs just a little onto the plate or bread, or if you are serving it on top of a salad, it makes a nice little pool of egg with the dressing on the bottom of the bowl.

Soft-Scrambled Eggs

1 teaspoon unsalted butter

2 large eggs

Sea salt

Melt the butter in a nonstick skillet over medium heat. Break the eggs into pan when it is warm but not yet hot. Sprinkle the eggs lightly with salt.

Let the pan heat up, and don't move the eggs until the egg whites begin to set. Using a rubber spatula, move the whites around the pan to help them cook through, while keeping the yolk unbroken. When the whites fluff up and are almost completely set, remove from the heat and fold the yolks into the whites. The residual heat should cook the whites through and leave the yolks soft. This is kind of like scrambling an over-easy egg.

To emphasize: Be careful not to overcook the eggs. Err on the side of runny rather than dry.

Cooking eggs sunny-side up can be an elusive art. The technique holds the allure of a perfect, unmangled egg with a virtually guaranteed nice runny yolk.

For this challenge, I like to make sure my attention is entirely on cooking the egg; there is a perfect moment that I am devoted to finding each time. It's a task that takes only minutes to perform, but it is totally engaging.

There are three approaches to the fried egg that I have come to rely on. The most foolproof method I know for creating a perfect sunny-side-up egg (pictured on page 65, bottom) is to place it in a warm pan with olive oil briefly, then transfer it to a hot oven until the white sets. For the classic skillet method, I alternate between the methods detailed below.

I fry my eggs in extra-virgin olive oil, but you can certainly use butter.

Sunny Eggs Three Ways

2 large eggs

1 to 2 tablespoons extra-virgin olive oil

MAKES 1 SERVING

For an oven-fried sunny egg, preheat the oven to 400°F. Heat the olive oil in an ovenproof skillet over medium heat. When the oil is warm but not hot, crack the eggs gently into the pan and cook without disturbing just until the white starts to set, about 1 minute. Transfer to the oven and bake just until the white sets completely, about 3 minutes longer.

For a quick-fried sunny egg, coat a skillet with the olive oil, place over medium heat, and carefully crack the eggs into the pan. When you start to hear the eggs sputtering, turn the heat down to low until you don't hear it anymore. If you hear sputtering again, reduce the heat a little more. Cook until set, about 5 minutes.

For a slow-fried sunny egg, put the pan over low heat with the olive oil and eggs, and just wait patiently for the eggs to heat and cook through, about 8 minutes. I like to tilt the pan to shimmy the egg into the curve at the edge and then tip it up again, so the egg coddles in the oil and cooks evenly. I also like to use a spoon to baste the whites for the same purpose.

Whichever way you like to cook them, serve your sunny eggs right away.

There are many opinions on the proper technique for boiling an egg; I myself have had many in this very life-time. The following slightly unusual approach, which yields a delicious result (pictured on facing page, left) was suggested to us (or rather, imposed upon us) by Stephen Tanner, who now makes his celebrated country food a few doors down at the Commodore. This method may seem dubious, as it did to me at first, because it requires a thumbtack. I have come to agree that it works best, particularly with noncommercial, pastured eggs—which are a little trickier to boil and peel.

It would seem that there is also something known as an egg piercer, which will perform the same function as the thumbtack without the concern that the tack might end up in the salad one day. We continue to use a tack and keep it housed in a plastic pint container.

Hard-Boiled Eggs

Kosher salt

6 to 12 large eggs

MAKES · 6-12 · HARD-BOILED EGGS

Bring a pot of well-salted water to a boil. Have ready a large bowl of ice water.

Meanwhile, using a thumbtack or an egg piercer, pierce the larger, rounded end of each egg by gently pushing and turning the thumbtack at the same time until the plastic "cap" of the tack touches the shell. Remove the tack.

When the water is boiling, quickly add the eggs. Boil for exactly 10 minutes. It is important to get the time right; you want the egg yolks to be bright orange and creamy, not dull and dry.

Using a slotted spoon, lift the eggs out of the water and plunge them into the ice bath. Let cool briefly. Don't let them stand for too long, or they will become difficult to peel. To peel, bang the bottom of the egg against the bowl so that it cracks and loosens up, then peel the shell away, making sure to get under the membrane that will cling to the white. (I like to keep the egg submerged under water while peeling, believing that the water seeping in assists in the peeling.) Remove from the ice bath and use right away, or store the peeled eggs in the refrigerator, covered, for up to 1 week.

Rebecca likes to try to make the pickled eggs the same color as the yolks—hence the turmeric. Use the eggs quickly, as they will get hard and rubbery if they sit for too many days in the pickle. I suggest having some pickle brine ready—it will keep, tightly covered in the refrigerator, for up to 2 months—and pickling only as many eggs as you know you will be eaten within 2 days. Slice to use in sandwiches such as The Captain's Daughter (page 100) or serve whole as an accompaniment to cocktails or a beer, like they do at an old beer-soaked bar where you're too afraid to order one.

Pickled Eggs

6 to 12 hard-boiled eggs, peeled (see page 64)

2 cups cider vinegar

2 cups water

¼ cup sugar

¼ cup kosher salt

About 1 tablespoon mixed pickling spices: equal parts coriander seeds, fennel seeds, mustard seeds, whole black peppercorns

1 teaspoon ground turmeric

MAKES 6-12 PICKLED EGGS

Put the eggs in a bowl or container with a tight-fitting lid. Set aside.

In a large saucepan, combine the vinegar, water, sugar, and salt and bring to a boil over high heat, stirring to dissolve the sugar and salt. Remove from the heat and add the spices and turmeric. Let the pickle cool completely, then pour it over the hard-boiled eggs. They should be fully submerged. Cover the bowl with plastic wrap or snap on the lid and let the eggs sit in the pickle in the refrigerator overnight. Serve within 2 days.

IT'S A TIGHT SHIP

387·4777

HOURS 10-6
CLOSED MONDAYS

Pickles

We are picklers. Herb pickers and picklers. I suppose if we didn't have a sandwich shop, perhaps we wouldn't spend so many of our working hours pickling. But pickle we do and must. A pickle brings a crunchy, acidic note to a sandwich that can otherwise become heavy and dull. Pickles have tremendous value in the kitchen whether sandwiched, eaten on their own, or added to other preparations to liven things up. Curries, meats, sauces, pâtes, and cured meats all benefit from the addition of a pickle. I am quite certain that no matter what we may do hereafter, pickles will come with us.

At Saltie, we use two basic pickling techniques: quick refrigerator pickling and fermentation. Our labor is divided according to the technique: Rebecca and I make refrigerator pickles; Elizabeth ferments. We go through a lot of pickles, so most of the pickles we make are the quick pickles, ready to eat a day after making them yet still holding well in the refrigerator for a month.

"Quick pickles" are vinegar based, rather than fermented pickles that rely on the action of lactobacteria. This means many things in terms of the differences between the two both nutritionally and technically. Refrigerator pickles are bright and vinegary, more of what we associate with pickles in jars. Fermented pickles are livelier and a little heavier but also crunchier, denser, and an important source of probiotics.

Refrigerator Pickles

The basic ratio that we use for these pickles is one part water to one part vinegar, with about twice the amount of sugar to salt and a mix of spices. This is only a template, and I encourage you to experiment, altering the recipe to your taste or to the subject to be pickled.

These pickles are not very sweet; if a sweeter pickle is desired—and many vegetables, like beets and carrots, are tasty sweeter—add more sugar. Also, experiment with different herbs and spices. I have found that with pickles, like everything else, there is no absolute best method. Rather, it is important to taste the pickling liquid and adjust the seasoning. In the end they should be balanced, not too vinegary, salty, or sweet.

Note that with many of the following pickle recipes, we call for arbol chile. This is a Mexican chile that imparts heat and great flavor. It is our preferred hot red chile, superior to red pepper flakes.

This is my attempt at a classic dill pickle. Many years ago I found a pickling book printed in 1965 that sparked my interest in the subject. This recipe was the most straightforward of the classic Kirby preparations in the book. (Although I admit, out of laziness, I have always omitted the step for icing down the Kirbys before pickling that would probably make a better pickle. Still, this is a good recipe.)

Dill flower is essential for creating the classically dill flavor that we associate with these pickles. Dill seed bought in a jar will not lend the same unmistakable quality but will do if there is no chance of finding the flower. The flower is simply the container for the seed of the dill plant. Any farmer who grows dill should have dill flower. We put the whole thing, stalk and flower, into the jar with the Kirbys.

Dill Pickles

2 dozen Kirby cucumbers, scrubbed and cut in half lengthwise

4 cups cider vinegar

4 cups water

1 cup sugar

½ cup kosher salt

½ cup garlic cloves, cut in half lengthwise

4 stalks fresh dill flower

2 small fresh chiles, such as jalapeño or serrano (preferably red), sliced in half lengthwise, or 2 to 4 dried arbol chiles or 1 tablespoon red pepper flakes

About 2 tablespoons mixed pickling spices: equal parts whole coriander, mustard seeds, whole allspice, whole cloves, whole black peppercorns

Put the cucumbers in a large heatproof bowl and set aside.

In a saucepan, combine the vinegar, water, sugar, and salt and bring to a boil over medium-high heat, stirring to dissolve the sugar and salt. When the sugar and salt have dissolved, pour the pickle over the cucumbers. Add the garlic, dill, chiles, and pickling spices to the bowl and stir to mix.

Let the pickles cool at room temperature and then put them into a plastic or glass container, cover, and refrigerate for at least 2 days or up to 1 week before serving. The dill pickles are ready when they are uniformly pickled, with no opaque rawness remaining, and will keep for up to 1 month.

MAKES 4 QUARTS

The seasonings here will make the pickle mildly curried.
You can also use the Dill Pickle recipe (see page 71) for
green tomatoes, if you don't want the curry flavor.

Curried Pickled Green Tomatoes

6 to 8 green tomatoes, cored
and cut into slices ¼ inch thick

1 large Spanish onion,
thinly sliced

2 cups cider vinegar

2 cups water

1 cup sugar

⅓ cup kosher salt

2 tablespoons each: coriander
seeds, fennel seeds, mustard
seeds, whole black peppercorns

2 teaspoons ground turmeric

1 tablespoon whole fenugreek

2 arbol chiles, crushed

Put the tomatoes and onion in a large heatproof bowl
and set aside.

In a saucepan, combine the vinegar, water, sugar,
salt, and whole spices and bring to a boil over medium-
high heat, stirring to dissolve the sugar and salt. When the
sugar and salt have dissolved, pour the pickle over
the tomatoes and onions. Add the turmeric, fenugreek,
and chiles and stir to mix. Taste. If pickle needs more
sugar or salt, adjust the seasoning. Look at the color of
the pickle; if you want it to be a deeper yellow, add more
turmeric, but be careful not to add too much, or it will
become bitter.

Let the pickles cool at room temperature and then
put them into a plastic or glass container, cover, and
refrigerate. The pickled green tomatoes will be ready
to eat the next day and will keep for up to 2 months.

These are the pickles that have caused our customers to ask for the Scuttlebutt (page 92) not by name but as "the sandwich with the beets on it." People love beets! Go figure. Here's what they are talking about.

Pickled Beets

2 bunches beets (about 10 beets, or 5 pounds total weight), scrubbed and trimmed

¼ cup olive oil

1 tablespoon kosher salt

2 cups red wine vinegar

2 cups water

1 cup sugar

½ tablespoon kosher salt

1 tablespoon whole black peppercorns

1 tablespoon coriander seeds

1 tablespoon mustard seeds

2 whole star anise, broken up

8 whole allspice berries

Preheat the oven to 400°F.

Put the beets in a roasting pan. Add just enough water to the pan to evenly cover the bottom. Salt the beets and drizzle with olive oil. Cover with aluminum foil and roast until tender when pierced with a knife, about an hour, depending on the size. Let cool until you can handle them, then peel the beets, slipping the skins off with your fingers or a kitchen towel and using a paring knife where they stick. Cut into slices ¼ inch thick and put in a large, heatproof bowl.

In a saucepan, combine the vinegar, water, sugar, salt, and spices and bring to a boil over medium-high heat, stirring to dissolve the sugar and salt. When the sugar and salt have dissolved, pour the pickle over the beets.

Let the pickles cool at room temperature and then put them into a plastic or glass container, cover, and refrigerate. The pickled beets will be ready to eat the next day and will keep for up to 2 months.

VARIATION: PICKLED RED ONIONS
Follow the main recipe, substituting 4 large red onions, thinly sliced, for the beets.

This is Tom Mylan's recipe from back when he was still the Grocery Guy. The old Tom—blogger, fermenter, distiller, bodega chef, knife collector, obsessive DIY'er—was the buyer for the specialty-food shop that was Marlow & Sons before he was sent to butcher boot camp, put in charge of the emerging whole-animal program at Diner and Marlow, and relocated to a tiny outdoor walk-in behind the restaurants. Today, Tom is Brooklyn's most famous butcher, but before that he was putting up his house-made bitters and hot sauce in every corner of the store.

Pickled Jalapeños

24 jalapeño chiles

2 tablespoons kosher salt

6 garlic cloves

2 cups apple cider vinegar, or as needed

Preheat the oven to 400°F.

Spread the jalapeños on a baking sheet and roast until they begin to blister and wilt, about 10 minutes. Let cool slightly, then transfer to quart-size jars. Add the salt and garlic to the jars and pour in the cider vinegar; it should just cover the jalapeños.

Let the pickles cool uncovered at room temperature. Then screw the lid on and place them in the refrigerator to let sit for at least 1 week before using. When you are ready to use the jalapeños, remove however many you need from the cider vinegar, pull off the stems, cut the peppers in half lengthwise, and scrape out the seeds. Chop the peppers and serve in sandwiches or in a small jar or bowl with a little of their pickling liquid. Replace the lid and store the remaining pickles in the refrigerator for up to 2 months.

VARIATION: PICKLED JALAPEÑO HOT SAUCE
To turn the pickles into hot sauce, stem and seed as many chiles as you need. Put in a blender or food processor with all the garlic and process to a smooth purée, adding back just enough pickling liquid to achieve the proper consistency. Taste and season with salt as necessary. You should get about 1 cup of hot sauce from 6 to 8 chiles.

These pickles are particularly great in The Balmy (page 108) and on the Clean Slate (page 84). We cut them into matchsticks once they are pickled to make them easier to mix into the sandwiches.

Carrot Pickle

8 medium carrots, peeled

2 cups apple cider vinegar

2 cups water

1 cup sugar

½ cup kosher salt

1 tablespoon coriander seeds

1 tablespoon fennel seeds

2 arbol chiles

Slice the carrots as thinly as possible, either into rounds or on the diagonal (bias). Put in a large heatproof bowl.

In a saucepan, combine the vinegar, water, sugar, salt, spices, and chiles and bring to a boil over medium-high heat, stirring to dissolve the sugar and salt. When the sugar and salt have dissolved, pour the pickle over the carrots.

Let the pickles cool at room temperature and then put them into a plastic or glass container, cover, and refrigerate. The carrot pickle will be ready to eat the next day and will keep for up to 2 months.

This pickle is more of a chutney. We serve it with the Curried Rabbit (page 87) and the East India Trade Chicken (page 107), both of which are curry-based dishes. It works well with rich preparations and is great with chicken, duck, or pork.

Currant Pickle

2 cups currants

2 teaspoons mustard seeds

1 tablespoon fresh thyme

1 cup sherry vinegar

¼ cup granulated sugar

¼ cup brown sugar

In a large saucepan, combine the currants, mustard seeds, thyme, vinegar, and both sugars and bring to a boil over medium-high heat. Lower the heat and simmer gently, stirring, until the sugar dissolves and the vinegar cooks off, making the whole thing reduced and sticky, about 30 minutes. Let cool.

The currant pickle will keep, stored in an airtight container in the refrigerator, for up to 2 months.

Fermented Pickles

Fermented foods are living foods that have been left open to the bacterial world to be transformed. Fermentation can be an intimidating notion. For years I wouldn't go near it. I was very happy and comfortable just making vinegar-based refrigerator pickles. Elizabeth, over the course of many years, has mastered fermentation and taught the rest of us how to do it. I cannot impress upon you enough how easy and rewarding fermented pickles are to make. They provide one of the few opportunities we have to witness beneficial bacteria at work transforming raw food into something else entirely, with health benefits that, while mysterious, cannot be underestimated. Spend some time fermenting and you will understand that you are not living alone and that life itself is much bigger and more interesting than you realize.

You will, however, need to set yourself up to ferment at home. In a perfect world, you have a ceramic fermenting crock with a lid. Otherwise, all this requires is a couple of large glass jars. The following recipes call for gallon-size glass jars to hold the vegetable for fermenting and quart-size jars to be placed inside the larger jar to weigh down the items during the process.

To review—you will need one 1-gallon glass jar and one 1-quart glass jar per batch of pickle. You also will need a clean kitchen towel and either a large rubber band or a roll of twine.

Sauerkraut is the easiest and most foolproof of the lacto-fermented breed of pickle. It generally behaves and tastes just as you would hope. Start with this to get your confidence up and then advance to the rest.

Sauerkraut

2 large heads red, green, or savoy cabbage

¼ cup sea salt

2 tablespoons pickling spices: caraway seeds, lightly crushed juniper berries, whole black peppercorns (choose one variety; don't mix)

MAKES
2-3
QUARTS

Cut the cabbages in quarters and cut out the cores. Lay the cut cabbage pieces flat on a cutting board and slice thinly. Place all the cabbage in a very large bowl and sprinkle with the sea salt and the spices. Toss to mix well.

Transfer the cabbage to a bucket or a stockpot and begin to pound it with the butt end of a rolling pin or other blunt pounding instrument. I know this sounds strange, but you want to break the cabbage down and get it to release its water. This will also compress the cabbage and assist in moving the fermentation along faster. You can stop pounding when the cabbage begins to turn a little translucent and is about half its original bulk.

Pack the cabbage tightly into a 1-gallon glass jar. Place a 1-quart glass jar filled with water inside the larger jar to weigh down the cabbage. Place a kitchen towel over both jars and secure it around the opening of the larger jar with a rubber band or twine. Place in a cool place away from direct sunlight. By the next day, the cabbage should be submerged in its own liquid. (If it isn't, make a brine by combining 1 cup water with 1 scant tablespoon sea salt and pour it over the cabbage. The cabbage will start to bubble and ferment quickly.)

Begin tasting the sauerkraut after 1 week and decide whether it needs to ferment longer. Sauerkraut is ready when it no longer has any rawness to it and the cabbage is dense and translucent. At this point, remove any goo or mold from around the top (don't be freaked out), transfer the sauerkraut to a clean glass jar, and refrigerate, tightly covered, for up to 2 months.

Elizabeth believes that the key to keeping these pickles crunchy is to pickle them on the day they are picked. This might require that you grow the Kirbys yourself. But if you buy them at a farmers' market, it's likely that they will be close to this fresh. Likewise, the grape leaves are intended to aid in keeping cukes crunchy. Sometimes you can find them at farmers' markets or an exceptional produce store, but you may need your own vines to find grape leaves, or if you live in a neighborhood like ours, just ask your Italian neighbor.

Fermented Cucumber Pickles

6 tablespoons sea salt

8 cups water

4 pounds Kirby cucumbers

1 bunch fresh grape leaves (optional)

2 stalks flowering dill

1 tablespoon whole black peppercorns

1 arbol chile, crumbled

1 head garlic, papery outer skin removed and cut in half

In a large bowl or a pitcher, make a brine by dissolving the sea salt in the water. Scrub the cucumbers well. Use your thumbnail or a paring knife to scrape away the blossom ends. Put the cucumbers in a bowl of ice water for about 1 hour to refresh them.

If you have access to fresh grape leaves, use them to line the bottom of two 1-gallon glass jars (unless you have one very large glass jar or crock). Add half the dill, peppercorns, chile, and garlic to each jar. Pack the cucumbers into the jars and pour in the brine to cover. Place a 1-quart jar filled with water inside each larger jar to weigh down the cucumbers. Place a kitchen towel over each jar and secure it around the opening of the larger jars with a rubber band or twine. Place in a cool place away from direct sunlight.

Check on the pickles daily, skimming away any mold that rises to the top, and begin tasting after a few days. Kirbys will usually take about 1 week to fully ferment. When they are ready, the Kirbys will be uniformly green and will no longer have any rawness about them. Transfer the pickles to clean glass jars and refrigerate, tightly covered, for up to 2 months.

focaccia

CHAPTER 2

SANDWICHES

My mother was not a sandwich lover. Despite that, she made my sister and me a brown-bagged sandwich every day for school lunch until it became painfully uncool and we begged her to stop. Nor was she a morning person—her efforts were better directed at dinnertime. We had one of two sandwiches, either Land O'Lakes American cheese and mayonnaise on white bread (our idea) or toasted white bread with Polly-O mozzarella (hers). Not a tomato slice or a leaf of lettuce grazed our daily take of cheese and bread—not because we wanted it that way, but because that's what she made. One day she made my sister Jackie a lunch of two pieces of toast wrapped in wax paper. Maybe what I do can be considered rebellion, taking everything I love to eat and putting it between two pieces of bread.

When I first started cooking at Savoy, in 1994, there was a sandwich shop in SoHo called Melampo. It was run by an Italian guy named Alessandro, and there was always a long line out the door. In this case it seemed that the line was due in part to the popularity of his shop and in part because it was just him, and he worked very slowly. He was also rather grumpy. The shop was a long, narrow space. On one side, the side where you lined up, there were shelves filled with imported Italian treats. On the other side, the wall was decorated with Italian movie posters, Fellini and Antonioni.

It was a shop where the owner's tastes and preferences were on display, further emphasized with a notice posted of behavioral do's and don'ts: Stay in line, don't wander around the shop, wait quietly for your sandwich, and above all don't try to alter any of the sandwiches in any way to suit your taste. If Alessandro liked you, which he might on one visit but not the next, he would put a little treat in your bag, a Perugina chocolate or a cookie of some sort. If he felt like talking, he would tell you a story, which meant he stopped working and it would take even longer to get your lunch while you stood there hoping you wouldn't say or do anything stupid and blow the whole thing.

Once you got your sandwich, there was nowhere to eat. You either had to take your sandwich with you or eat it at the playground next door. I liked to eat at the playground, which seemed like the perfect way to complement the experience, eating among loud, disorderly children. I thought about how nice it would be to own a little sandwich shop. It seemed romantic to do a simple and wonderful thing the same way every day. I have always had a fondness for sandwiches, but this place, and this Italian guy, made me realize there was something magical about them, too. It seemed to me that sandwiches made people happy. Since then I have come to understand that often our greatest culinary experiences are the little unexpected ones— when something you eat corresponds directly to how you feel in your heart.

Undoubtedly, the number-one question we get asked is, "What's the most popular sandwich?" That's easy: It's the Scuttlebutt. The second is, "How did you come up with the sandwiches?" This one always makes me pause and wonder. Are they really so exotic? So original? Doesn't everyone think of these things when they think of a sandwich? It feels like from the very moment we sat down to formalize the menu, these flavors and combinations were obvious, waiting for us. So we tell the curious that the sandwich menu came together in a matter of minutes—as if handed to us on a divine tablet. Of course these sandwiches are also the culmination of many years of work, and of working together. We all speak the same language and like the same things. Our creative collaboration has always been one of finishing each other's sentences, walking in with exactly the same idea about something new. Working together in this way has been easy. We are lucky to have each other.

This sandwich is dedicated to my friend Joe, to whom I once sent out a plate of spring onion sandwiches as a little starter course for him and his friends dining at Marlow. As soon as I placed them down I realized that maybe this wasn't the right crowd for raw onions and mayonnaise. I felt their suspicion, as though I had lost all good sense, smiles fixed and eyes questioning. While they were admittedly skeptical, they were obligated to try. My initial judgment—that right now there was nothing more delicious than this sandwich—triumphed. Joe asks for them every June.

This recipe is adapted from *Chez Panisse Vegetables*. In that book, Alice Waters talks about how she borrowed her recipe from James Beard—illustrating again that these things go 'round and 'round and 'round.

Spring onions start out looking like scallions. As the season progresses they get bigger, forming their oniony bulb. Spring onions can be either green or purple; choosing one over the other is largely aesthetic.

Alice Waters's Spring Onion Sandwich
Spring onions, mayonnaise, chives, lemon juice

1 sandwich-size piece of Focaccia (page 36)

3 tablespoons mayonnaise, preferably homemade (see page 44)

6 spring onions, thinly sliced on the diagonal (bias)

1 tablespoon minced fresh chives

Extra-virgin olive oil

Fresh lemon juice

Sea salt

Cut the focaccia in half horizontally and put on a plate, cut-sides up. Spread both cut sides with the mayonnaise and set aside.

In a bowl, toss the spring onions and chives together with a drizzling of olive oil, a sprinkling of lemon juice, and a pinch of salt.

Mound the onion mixture on the bottom half of the bread, then replace the top and press lightly to help the sandwich hold together. I like to serve this as more of a finger sandwich, so I cut it into quarters. Serve right away.

Like the Romaine Dinghy (page 102), the Walty is a seasonal sandwich built around a vegetable that's about to be slathered in mayonnaise. As the anchovy is the surprise ingredient in the Dinghy, the green coriander seed is the hero of the Walty. In fact, it's arguable that this sandwich came to be because of green coriander. Coriander is the seed of the cilantro plant. When it's fresh, it's green. Later it will turn brown and dry out, becoming the coriander that we recognize on the spice rack. The green seed contains all that is wonderful about both cilantro and coriander. It's the perfect expression of both.

Green coriander seed, like dill seed, is the seed contained in the flower of the plant. Grow it, buy it at the farmers' market, or if you can't find it, use dried and add some cilantro to the recipe.

Walty

Cucumber, green coriander seeds, arbol chile, fresh mint, mayonnaise

1 tablespoon fresh green coriander seeds

1 arbol chile

1 medium cucumber (choose a cucumber that's not too big, or else it will be all seeds)

1 tablespoon roughly chopped fresh mint

Sea salt

Extra-virgin olive oil

White wine vinegar

1 sandwich-size piece of Focaccia (page 36)

3 tablespoons mayonnaise, preferably homemade (see page 44)

MAKES 1 SANDWICH

Pound the coriander seeds and chile together with a mortar and pestle.

Cut the rounded ends off the cucumber and then peel it with a vegetable peeler, creating alternating stripes of the green peel and the peeled white flesh of the cucumber. Slice the cucumber into rounds as thinly as possible. (You will probably need only half or maybe two-thirds of the cucumber for the one sandwich, but you may as well go ahead and prepare the whole thing.) It's important that the slices are thin, or else the sandwich will not stack easily.

In a bowl, toss the sliced cucumber with 1 teaspoon of the ground coriander and the chile mixture along with the mint, a pinch of sea salt, a drizzle of olive oil, and a splash of white wine vinegar. Let sit at room temperature to marinate and wilt for about 5 minutes.

Cut the focaccia in half horizontally and put on a plate, cut-sides up. Spread both cut sides with the mayonnaise. Carefully stack the cucumbers on the bottom half of the bread, arranging them in overlapping layers as you go. Stop stacking when you have about 2 inches of cucumber. Replace the top of the bread and press lightly to help the sandwich hold together. Serve right away.

"It's a kind of probiotic wonder." —ES

The Clean Slate was conceived of as a sort of semi-macrobiotic, complete protein sandwich. A sandwich that contains what we all believe to be the basic ingredients of good health—grains, beans, fermented vegetables, yogurt, and seeds. This sandwich was born from a lunch that Elizabeth made for us when we were still under construction. Tired of eating pizza and deli sandwiches, she brought in leftovers from her dinner the night before. It was immediately apparent that if we were to stuff those leftovers inside of a piece of oily naan, we would have a sandwich that could satisfy both the desire to be healthy and the desire to eat well.

Clean Slate
Hummus, quinoa, yogurt sauce, sauerkraut, sesame seeds

The Clean Slate, much like the Scuttlebutt (page 92), is a kind of choose-your-own-adventure sandwich. You can add anything reasonable to it as long as you have the basics in place, which are hummus, grain, yogurt sauce, some sort of pickled vegetable, and sesame seeds. You can make the hummus with red lentils or other beans, or substitute bulgur wheat or brown rice for quinoa. The quantities listed here for each ingredient can be altered to taste as well.

We use miso in our hummus, because it assists in making the chickpeas more digestible and provides some probiotics and a little je-ne-sais-quoi *umami*. Quinoa, hailed as a supergrain, is light, fluffy, and nutty, with a bit of a crunch. Choose red quinoa if possible—I find it to be less bitter than the yellow and better looking, too.

FOR THE HUMMUS

1 teaspoon coriander seeds

1 teaspoon cumin seeds

4 garlic cloves

2 cups cooked, drained chickpeas

2 tablespoons tahini

2 teaspoons red miso (optional)

¼ cup fresh lemon juice

¼ cup extra-virgin olive oil

Sea salt

FOR THE QUINOA

1 cup quinoa

1½ cups water

1 teaspoon salt

1 piece warm Naan (page 40)

2 to 3 tablespoons Yogurt Sauce (page 55)

Sauerkraut (page 78) and/or other pickles for topping

2 tablespoons shredded raw carrots or chiffonade of greens

1 tablespoon roughly chopped fresh mint, cilantro, and/or dill

1 teaspoon toasted sesame seeds

TO MAKE THE HUMMUS, in a small, dry skillet over medium heat, toast the coriander and cumin seeds, stirring constantly, until fragrant, about 1 minute. Pound with a mortar and pestle. Transfer to a food processor and add the garlic, chickpeas, tahini, and miso (if using) to the bowl and process until well blended. Add the lemon juice, olive oil, and a pinch of sea salt and process until smooth. Taste and adjust the seasoning. Set aside.

TO MAKE THE QUINOA, rinse the grains in a fine-mesh sieve (this will remove the bitterness). Transfer to a saucepan and add the water and salt. Bring to a boil over high heat, then cover and reduce the heat to maintain a simmer. Cook until all of the water has been absorbed, 10 to 15 minutes. Remove from the heat and let the cooked quinoa rest in the pot to steam and cool.

Place the naan on a plate and spread the center of it evenly with ¼ cup of the hummus, leaving an inch around the edge without hummus. Place ¼ cup of the quinoa on top of the hummus and spread it evenly across the bread, but just short of the edges of the hummus. Drizzle yogurt sauce over the quinoa and hummus and then top with sauerkraut (and/or other pickles), carrots, herbs, sesame seeds, and so on. Fold the Clean Slate in half and eat it like a big taco.

This recipe is for 1 sandwich, but you won't use all of the hummus and quinoa. Store leftovers in airtight containers in the refrigerator for up to 5 days.

NOTE: It's also not a bad idea to use a little hot sauce or Pickled Jalapeño (page 74) here. I love hot sauce, but it should be used judiciously. There is a time and a place for hot sauce, but . . . used on everything? You have only the taste of hot sauce! At some point the entire nuance is lost to the condiment. Don't become addicted to hot sauce, or ketchup (or girls, or beer).

Like the Henry Hudson (page 106), here's a sandwich that proves how consistently good fried vegetables and mayonnaise are together. And in this case, *fried* vegetables, mayonnaise, and mozzarella. At first I thought that the combination of mayonnaise and mozzarella might go against a principle instilled in me by Anne Fidanza—that these two ingredients are not friends. Contrary to what she might think, they most certainly are.

Also, as with the Henry Hudson, this sandwich is best eaten when the zucchini is first fried, but you can reheat the zucchini in a 350°F oven.

Italian-American
Fried zucchini, tomato, mozzarella, pesto, mayonnaise

2 large eggs

½ cup all-purpose flour

½ cup cornmeal

Kosher salt

1 large zucchini, cut on the diagonal into slices about ¼ inch thick

Olive oil for frying

2 sandwich-size pieces of Focaccia (page 36)

4 tablespoons mayonnaise, preferably homemade (see page 44)

1 ball fresh mozzarella, thinly sliced

1 large tomato, sliced

2 tablespoons basil pesto, preferably homemade (see page 50)

MAKES 2 SANDWICHES

Break the eggs into a shallow bowl and whisk to blend. Put the flour and cornmeal in two separate shallow bowls. Add a pinch of salt to both the flour and cornmeal and stir to combine.

Dredge each slice of zucchini first in the flour, then the beaten egg, then the cornmeal. Set the breaded zucchini aside on a platter or baking sheet.

Heat a large cast-iron skillet over medium-high heat and pour in enough olive oil to cover the bottom of the pan evenly. When the oil is hot, add some of the breaded zucchini in a single layer. Do not crowd the pan. Cook, turning once, until golden brown on both sides, about 2 minutes per side. When the zucchini are done, transfer to a plate lined with paper towels and sprinkle with salt while they are still hot. Repeat to cook all of the zucchini.

Cut the focaccia in half horizontally and put on a plate, cut-sides up. Spread both cut sides with the mayonnaise. Place 2 or 3 pieces of zucchini on each bottom half of the bread, followed by 2 slices of mozzarella and 2 slices of tomato. Spread the pesto on top of the tomato. Replace the tops of the bread and press lightly to help the sandwich hold together. Serve right away.

There is no actual rabbit here. This cheesy sandwich is a variation on Welsh rarebit, also commonly called Welsh rabbit, which is basically a melted cheese sandwich. Approximately 1 percent of our customers get the reference and the wink. More often, as with most of our jokes, it goes go unnoticed. Sometimes I wonder why we choose to make things so complicated. Sometimes we can't resist.

Rebecca, in her quest for curry and her love of vinegar and pickley things, conceived of this addictive combination. The Currant Pickle is not a requirement for this dish but certainly makes it a much more complete experience. As with all rich, fatty dishes, it's nice to have an acidic element, in this case a fruity one, to balance it out. Branston pickle, an English chutney that can be found in good specialty shops, would be a traditional accompaniment to this sandwich. We complete the dish with an apple salad.

Curried Rabbit

Cheddar, curried mayonnaise, apple salad, currant pickle

2 ounces sharp Cheddar cheese, shredded

2 tablespoons Curried Mayonnaise (page 45)

1 sandwich-size piece of Focaccia (page 36) (a nice rye bread would also be in order here)

1 apple, cored and thinly sliced

1 teaspoon minced fresh parsley

Juice of ½ lemon

Dash of extra-virgin olive oil

Pinch of sea salt

Currant Pickle (page 76)

Preheat the broiler.

In a small bowl, combine the cheese and mayonnaise and stir to mix well.

Cut the focaccia in half horizontally and put on a baking sheet. Spread both cut sides with the cheese mixture. Place the sandwich halves, cheese-side up, under the broiler until the cheese melts and starts to bubble and brown, about 4 minutes. Remove from the oven and let cool slightly.

In another small bowl, combine the apple, parsley, lemon juice, olive oil, and sea salt. Arrange the sandwich open-faced on a plate, pile the apple salad and currant pickle alongside, and serve right away.

MAKES 1 SANDWICH

It's hard to fall in love with nettles, especially when they're all that God or Guy Jones has to give you. Nettles may be the first green to arrive each year, but each year, you are faced with having to coax them from their prickly, earthy constitution.

But when we came up with this dish, I did fall in love with them. This combination brings out their bright green, earthy minerality and natural sweetness. This is something I think of more as an egg dish than a sandwich. It's not something that you can pick up with your hands and eat. This sandwich is meant to be eaten with a knife and fork, so be generous with the sauce; it can and should pour over onto the plate.

Green Egg
Nettle sauce, sunny egg, pecorino

1 sandwich-size piece of Focaccia (page 36)

3 tablespoons Nettle Sauce (page 49), or more as desired

1 large egg

Sea salt

1 small piece (about 1 ounce) *pecorino toscano*, preferably 30-day aged

Freshly ground black pepper

Cut the focaccia in half horizontally. Put the bottom on a plate, cut-side up, and set the top aside. In a small pan over low heat, gently warm the nettle sauce.

Heat a nonstick skillet and fry the egg (see page 63). When the egg is cooked, spread the sauce generously on (and overflowing) the bottom half of the bread.

Place the egg on top of the nettle sauce and sprinkle sea salt lightly over all. Shave the pecorino over the egg and finish with a grind of black pepper. Serve right away, open-faced, placing the top piece of the focaccia on the side to dip in the egg and sauce.

"What one wants is the taste of the fresh eggs and the fresh butter. . . . It should not be a busy, important urban dish but something gentle and pastoral, with the clean scent of the dairy, the kitchen garden . . ."

—ELIZABETH DAVID

We knew we wanted to have an egg sandwich on the menu and that it should be as simple as an egg sandwich that you get at a diner or even a bodega. While in the recipe-testing phase for the focaccia, we decided to make egg sandwiches for ourselves for breakfast. The only cheese in the house was ricotta. A revelation.

There's not much to this sandwich, but it is creamy, light, and luxurious. The two important things here are the ricotta and the egg technique. It's not always easy to find good fresh ricotta. We use Calabro, made in East Haven, Connecticut. I have seen Calabro ricotta here and there in local retail markets. The ricotta available commercially on a national level is not very good. It's dry and grainy. If you can find a ricotta that is still a little wet, that's the best choice. Any good Italian market should have something better than what's available in the supermarket.

Ship's Biscuit
Soft-scrambled eggs, fresh ricotta

1 sandwich-size piece of Focaccia (page 36)

About 2 tablespoons fresh ricotta

2 large eggs

Coarse sea salt

Cut the focaccia in half horizontally and put the bottom half on a plate, cut-side up. Spread the ricotta in an even and generous layer on the cut side. Set aside.

Soft-scramble the eggs (see page 62) with a pinch of sea salt.

Spoon the eggs on top of the ricotta. Replace the top of the bread and serve right away.

"I'm English, and the Scuttlebutt is really a sandwich my sister used to make for me of salad on white bread with salad cream. . . . It's obviously tweaked a bit, but when we said, 'Oh, we're going to make sandwiches; what was your favorite sandwich?' I'd say I had this really awesome sandwich of hard-boiled eggs and whatever was in the fridge—a Dagwood Bumstead. It was really delicious."

—RC

There is so much to say about the Scuttlebutt. It really has earned its gossipy title. It's the sandwich that is most likely to change, as the ingredients rotate with the seasons and with what's in the refrigerator. In summer, it has tomatoes and arugula; in winter, squash and a chiffonade of Tuscan kale. There is a rotating cast of pickles,

Scuttlebutt

Hard-boiled egg, *pimentón* aioli, feta, black olive, capers, fresh herbs, pickled beets

1 sandwich-size piece of Focaccia (page 36)

2 tablespoons Pimentón Aioli (page 47)

1 hard-boiled egg (see page 64), peeled and sliced

1 tablespoon pitted oil-cured olives, chopped

½ tablespoon capers

¼ cup Fresh Herb Mix (page 58)

2 tablespoons chopped pickles, ideally Pickled Beets (page 73)

1 radish, thinly sliced (optional but nice)

Extra-virgin olive oil

1 ounce sheep's milk feta

the most popular being the beet. Some people order the Scuttlebutt as "the sandwich with the beets," which never fails to disappoint when those particular pickles are off the menu. The staple ingredients remain *pimentón* aioli, hard-boiled egg, feta, capers, and olives. The rest is a free-for-all that for some can end in tears. The Scuttlebutt makes people emotional. It is an exercise in impermanence.

Cut the focaccia in half horizontally and put on a plate, cut-sides up. Spread both cut sides with aioli. Arrange the egg slices evenly on the bottom half of the bread. Set aside.

In a bowl, toss the olives, capers, herbs, pickles, and radish (if using) with just enough olive oil to coat lightly. Mound the salad on top of the egg. If you can, slice the feta and arrange on top of the salad. If you can't get a nice even slice of feta, you can either crumble it on top of the salad (although it will tend to roll off the top of pile), or you can toss the feta with the salad. Quickly replace the top of the bread before the sandwich falls apart, pressing gently to help it hold together, and serve right away.

MAKES 1 SANDWICH

This sandwich began as Rebecca's snack. And every time she made it for herself, I would sulk—both because she didn't offer to make me one and because I probably just had thoughtlessly eaten something unremarkable so I wouldn't be hungry anymore. I would enviously watch her eat it with a knife and fork, so pleased with herself for finally remembering that she deserved something good.

The Town Ho
Pimentón aioli, fried egg

1 sandwich-size piece of
Focaccia (page 36)

3 tablespoons Pimentón Aioli
(page 47)

1 large egg

Sea salt

Cut the focaccia in half horizontally and put on a plate, cut-sides up. Spread both cut sides with the aioli. Set aside.

Heat a nonstick skillet and fry the egg (see page 63). When the egg is cooked, sprinkle it with sea salt and shimmy it onto the bottom piece of aioli-dressed bread. Replace the top and serve right away.

The Famous Bun is a cheeseburger, hold the burger. It's the sandwich that we ate in the kitchen at Diner when we were starving and wanted something delicious but had twenty seconds to throw it together and another minute to shovel it down. Irony of ironies, restaurant cooks don't have very much opportunity to eat. These ingredients are collectively the accoutrements of the burger—and arguably the best part.

The Famous Bun

Cheddar, red onion, lettuce, tomato, dill pickle, mayonnaise

1 sandwich-size piece of Focaccia (page 36)

2 tablespoons mayonnaise, preferably homemade (see page 44)

1 dill pickle, sliced lengthwise (we make our own; see page 71)

2 thick slices good sharp Cheddar

2 large leaves romaine or leaf lettuce

1 or 2 slices red onion

1 or 2 slices ripe tomato

Cut the focaccia in half horizontally and put on a plate, cut-sides up. Spread both cut sides with the mayonnaise. Arrange the pickle on the bottom half of the bread and stack on the Cheddar, lettuce leaves, onion, and tomato. Replace the top and press lightly to help the sandwich hold together. Serve right away.

MAKES · 1 · SANDWICH

According to Rebecca, potato tortilla and nice white bread is a popular sandwich all over Spain. It's an enormous sandwich wrapped in foil, enough food for a day. We maintain the same spirit in our version.

The potato tortilla is one of the first dishes that I connected with on a deep level and mastered. I had to make it every day for a year when I first started cooking at Savoy. As a result, I am forever bound to it and have brought it along with me wherever I have gone. As these things go, the tortilla currently has a strong presence in Williamsburg. But I am confident that this one set the standard.

Spanish Armada
Potato tortilla and *pimentón* aioli

This is a recipe that requires the relatively tremendous effort of making a potato tortilla just in order to make a sandwich out of it. It's kind of backward, but in the most wonderfully excessive way. The Spanish Armada starts with something I already love dearly and then takes it to a place that is utterly illegal. It is bread, aioli, and potato. All you really need from this recipe is to learn how to make potato tortilla. Once understood, you will make it again and again; it's simply a great thing to know how to make. Beyond that, you can make a sandwich, or you can eat it as is with a little aioli, a salad, cured meats, or marinated vegetables. After all, it's a potato dish—it goes with nearly everything.

This recipe is for a large tortilla, which will easily serve 10 or 12 people. It's no small feat to produce a tortilla of this size, but I think it's just a wonderful thing to know how to make. It is quite impressive, with a beautiful striated structure and a lovely rounded form. Once mastered, it will be easy to cut the recipe down and make a smaller tortilla.

CONTINUED

TO MAKE THE TORTILLA, place a large cast-iron Dutch oven over low heat and pour in the olive oil. While the oil is warming slowly, peel the potatoes and slice them very thinly, about ⅛ inch thick. Do not rinse or hold the sliced potatoes in water. You need the starch later, to hold the tortilla together.

Raise the heat to medium and place a slice of potato in the warm oil. When the potato slice starts to bubble, carefully add the rest of the potatoes. Adjust the heat to cook the potatoes *slowly*—at a simmer, not a boil—stirring occasionally. While the potatoes are cooking, slice the onion in half, cutting it from top to bottom and then lengthwise into thin slices.

When the potatoes are still al dente but starting to soften, add the onion to the pot. Continue cooking until the potatoes are completely soft and the onion is translucent. It's okay if the potatoes start to fall apart—better to overcook them than to undercook them. When the potatoes are ready, strain them through a colander placed over a heatproof bowl. (Set the oil aside for now, because you will use a little a few steps later; then save the rest in an airtight container in the refrigerator for another use. It may be a little potatoey, but it's entirely usable and delicious.)

Put the potatoes and onion in a large bowl, season them generously with salt, and toss to mix. Let the mixture cool slightly. While it's still warm, break the eggs into the bowl. Do not prebreak and whisk—just break the eggs directly onto the potatoes. Once all the eggs are in, mix the eggs, potatoes, and onions well with a wooden spoon. Season additionally with salt. The potatoes will take a lot of salt, more than you may be comfortable with. Keep in mind that this is a lot of food, and potatoes always need a lot of salt. The mix should taste salty—not excessively, but it should really be there.

FOR THE TORTILLA

4 cups pure olive oil

10 medium Yukon gold potatoes (about 3 pounds total weight)

1 large Spanish onion

Kosher salt

12 large eggs

Focaccia (page 36)

Pimentón Aioli (page 47)

MAKES 10–12 SERVINGS

Place a 12-inch cast-iron skillet over high heat. Add back enough of the potato-cooking oil to evenly cover the bottom of the pan. When the oil is hot, slide the potato mixture into the skillet. Immediately reduce the heat to medium-low and jiggle the pan. Using a rubber spatula, go around the potato mixture, pushing the sides of the tortilla in. When the egg begins to set, again use the spatula to push against the sides of the tortilla, both shaping it and wiggling it to prevent it from sticking.

Once the edges of the tortilla seem nicely set, 20 to 30 minutes, flip the tortilla. This is the daunting (but fun) part. Find a flat lid larger in circumference than the skillet. Place the lid on top of the pan and flip the tortilla onto the lid. Put the skillet back onto the burner and slide the tortilla into the pan to finish cooking on the other side. At this point the tortilla is mostly cooked through; you are just finishing off the top (which you want to be more gold than brown). Again, go around the tortilla and push in the sides with the spatula to make sure that the finished tortilla will have a nicely rounded shape. Cook the tortilla on low heat for 5 minutes and then turn the heat off. Let the tortilla cool for about 5 minutes longer in the pan and then flip (AGAIN!) onto a serving platter.

Cut a sandwich-size piece of focaccia in half horizontally and put on a plate, cut-sides up. Spread each cut side with about 2 tablespoons of the aioli. Transfer the tortilla to a cutting board and cut into quarters. Working with one quarter, cut along one side to make two slices about ½ inch thick; they should be roughly the same length as the focaccia. Arrange the tortilla slices on the bottom half of the focaccia, then replace the top and serve. Repeat to make as many sandwiches as you need.

Serve at room temperature. Store any leftover tortilla, covered, at room temperature too. Do not reheat, or the tortilla will get dry.

The Captain's Daughter was the first Saltie sandwich to be conceived. It opened the gate through which all the other sandwiches passed.

We all have a similar affection for sardines. Canned sardines were the perfect answer to how to have a little fish on the menu. The fact that the people of this city appreciate a sardine as delicious makes me grateful every day.

There are plenty of sardines on the market. I like to use sardines from the Mediterranean. Generally brands from Spain, Portugal, Italy, or Morocco, packed in olive oil, are of superior quality. These may vary tremendously in price, so choose based on what seems reasonable. We use a can of sardines per sandwich, but it's quite possible that you may want to use less, depending on the size of your can of sardines, your sandwich, or your appetite.

The Captain's Daughter

Sardines, pickled egg, *salsa verde*

1 sandwich-size piece of Focaccia (page 36)

One 4-ounce can good-quality sardines, packed in olive oil

1 Pickled Egg (page 66)

¼ cup Salsa Verde (page 56)

Cut the focaccia in half horizontally and put on a plate, cut-sides up. Lift the sardines gently out of the can and separate into fillets. Arrange on the bottom half of the bread to cover the entire surface.

Slice the egg and arrange on top of the sardines. Mound the *salsa verde* on top of the egg. Replace the top of the bread and press lightly to help the sandwich hold together. Serve right away.

Here is a lettuce sandwich to herald the spring. I started thinking about this sandwich toward the end of our first winter at Saltie while daydreaming about what we could look forward to next. Anchovies bring a bit of brininess and edginess to this simple sandwich. The watery crunch of romaine with mayonnaise between two pieces of bread will keep me content all season.

Romaine Dinghy
Romaine lettuce, anchovy, radish, mayonnaise

1 sandwich-size piece of Focaccia (page 36)

2 tablespoons mayonnaise, preferably homemade (see page 44)

4 large romaine leaves

1 large red radish, thinly sliced

1 teaspoon chopped anchovy

1 teaspoon minced fresh chives

Juice of 1 lemon

1 tablespoon extra-virgin olive oil

Sea salt

Cut the focaccia in half horizontally and put on plate, cut-sides up. Spread both cut sides with the mayonnaise. Place the romaine leaves on a cutting board and slice them crosswise into three sections. Transfer to a large bowl and add the radish, anchovy, chives, lemon juice, olive oil, and a pinch of salt. Toss to mix and coat well.

Stack the romaine mixture neatly on the bottom half of the bread. Replace the top of the bread and press lightly to help the sandwich hold together. Serve right away.

Romaine
Dinghy

an
entire.
head of
romaine.

Henry Hudson.

We first served this sandwich in the late summer and fall of 2009, which coincided with the quadricentennial of the voyage of Henry Hudson up the river that now bears his name. This grand and popular sandwich was intended to honor his significance in the settlement and popular imagination of New York City.

Henry Hudson

Fried green tomatoes, bacon, mayonnaise, fresh basil

1 large green tomato

2 large eggs

½ cup flour

½ cup cornmeal

Kosher salt

Extra-virgin olive oil

2 sandwich-size pieces of Focaccia (page 36)

4 tablespoons mayonnaise, preferably homemade (see page 44)

12 fresh basil leaves

6 bacon strips, cooked until crisp

MAKES · 2 · SANDWICHES

Core the green tomato and cut into six slices about ¼ inch thick. Break the eggs into a bowl and whisk to blend. Place the flour and cornmeal in two separate small bowls or pans. Add a pinch of salt to both the flour and cornmeal and stir to combine. (You can add any other seasoning you like at this point, too—cayenne, paprika, etc.) Dredge each slice of tomato first in flour, then egg, then cornmeal.

Heat a large cast-iron skillet over medium-high heat and pour in enough olive oil to evenly cover the bottom of the pan. When the oil is hot, add a batch of tomatoes in a single layer. Cook, turning once, until golden brown on both sides, about 3 minutes per side. Transfer the tomatoes to a plate lined with paper towels and, while they are still hot, sprinkle them with salt. Repeat cooking in batches until all the tomatoes are cooked.

Cut the focaccia in half horizontally and put a top and bottom half, cut-side up, on each of two plates. Spread both cut sides with mayonnaise. Place a fried green tomato on the bottom half of each, followed by 2 basil leaves and 1 strip of bacon. Continue on stacking until you have three layers on each sandwich. Replace the tops of the bread and press lightly to help the sandwiches hold together. Serve right away.

East India Trade Chicken was our name for this rich chicken sandwich. Turns out that it's Coronation Chicken—the very chicken dish that was served to HRH the Queen on her coronation day! That's when you know you're plugged into the universe. The ingredients for this sandwich would also make a great cold main course, composed rather than mixed together and served alongside the butter lettuce.

East India Trade Chicken, a.k.a. Coronation Chicken
Poached chicken, curried mayonnaise, currant pickle

One 3½- to 4-pound chicken

2 cups Curried Mayonnaise (page 45)

½ cup Currant Pickle (page 76)

Sea salt

1 head butter lettuce (approximately 12 to 15 leaves)

1 teaspoon lemon juice

1 teaspoon extra-virgin olive oil

Focaccia (page 36), cut into sandwich-size pieces and cut in half horizontally

MAKES 6–8 SANDWICHES

Cook the chicken using the method for Cock-a-Leekie on page 137. Let cool.

Pull the chicken into 1-inch pieces and place them in a large bowl. Add the mayonnaise and currant pickle and stir to mix well. Taste for salt. Dress the lettuce leaves with lemon juice, olive oil, and a little sea salt. Pile chicken on the focaccia, top with lettuce, and serve right away.

One night, I was having dinner with our friend Gerard at a Vietnamese noodle-ish restaurant. I was excited to be there, in good company, eating flavors that I don't get often enough. Gerard was a phenomenal eater, one of those people who would impulsively travel to Queens to eat a sesame bun at a favorite Chinese restaurant. That evening, he assumed the role of cookbook coach, delivering me his copy of Fannie Farmer, saying only that I should read the introduction. I had never given much thought to this particular classic—and worse, probably dismissed it as irrelevant. I read the first paragraph at the table that night, and immediately put it aside, realizing that there was something too big in there to take in right then.

The Balmy

Chicken liver mousse; ham; pickled carrot, jalapeño, beet, and red onion; fresh cilantro; sesame seeds; mayonnaise

I still can't comprehend the magnitude of that introduction. The very first line—"Every meal should be a small celebration"—is all that needs to be said, forever. I was completely overcome, as I had been when I first read Elizabeth David or M. F. K. Fisher, moved by the fact that these authors, writing in some cases nearly a century ago, are so utterly timeless in both style and subject matter; their voices remain relevant, clear, and contemporary. For them, thinking and writing about cooking and eating was thinking and writing about life—the pleasures of and meditations on both are tightly woven together.

As we began to eat our dinner, I started thinking about expanding the palette of Saltie. Nudging it a little farther east. Gerard happily jumped in, and the Balmy was created.

This is our version of a *bánh mì*, a classic French-Vietnamese sandwich. Like the East India Trade Chicken, this sandwich serves as an example of the positive results of European imperialism.

CONTINUED

2 tablespoons Carrot Pickle
(page 75)

2 tablespoons Pickled Beets
(page 73)

2 tablespoons Pickled Red
Onions (page 73)

1 teaspoon seeded and minced
Pickled Jalapeño (page 74)

Equal parts fresh cilantro
leaves, fresh mint leaves,
and thinly sliced scallion,
¼ cup total

1 teaspoon toasted
sesame seeds

Sea salt

Extra-virgin olive oil

1 sandwich-size piece of
Focaccia (page 36)

3 tablespoons Chicken Liver
Mousse (recipe follows)

1 tablespoon mayonnaise,
preferably homemade
(see page 44)

3 slices cured and smoked ham
(see Note, page 117)

In a bowl, combine the pickled carrots, beets, red onions, and
jalapeño. Add the herbs, scallion, and sesame seeds and stir
to mix well. Season with sea salt, olive oil, and a teaspoon
or so of the jalapeño pickling liquid. Taste again and adjust
for salt and heat.

Cut the focaccia in half horizontally and put on a plate,
cut-sides up. Spread the chicken liver mousse evenly on
the cut side of the bottom half. Spread the mayonnaise on the
cut side of the top. Evenly layer three slices of ham on top
of the chicken liver. Place the salad of mixed pickled vegetables and herbs on top of the ham. Replace the top of the
bread and press lightly to help hold the sandwich together.
Serve right away.

Chicken Liver Mousse

This recipe for chicken liver mousse comes from our
friend and wondercook Nir Feller, whom we worked
with at Diner until he had to return to Israel. It will yield
more than the amount required to make a sandwich but
is ready to go and can be eaten on its own with toast or
crackers when you get home from work and don't want
to cook and have half a bottle of white wine in the fridge,
or if you want to impress someone and serve them this
as a snack or an appetizer. While making this recipe, do
not be afraid to add a lot of butter to the pan to cook the
livers and aromatics; that is where a lot of the flavor is
going to come from. This is not a low-cal, low-fat dish,
so you may as well make it taste as good as it can.

½ cup (1 stick) unsalted butter, plus 3 tablespoons

1 large Spanish onion, sliced

4 shallots, sliced

4 cloves garlic, sliced

1 tablespoon fresh thyme

2 whole star anise, broken up

Kosher salt

1 pound chicken livers

Freshly ground black pepper

Extra-virgin olive oil

Sherry vinegar

½ cup brandy

MAKES 1 PINT

In a large cast-iron skillet over medium heat, melt the ½ cup butter. Add the onion, shallots, garlic, thyme, and star anise, season well with salt, and stir to coat everything in the melted butter. Reduce the heat to medium-low and cook the mixture slowly, stirring occasionally, until deeply caramelized, about 30 minutes. Transfer to a large bowl and set aside. Wipe the pan clean and reserve.

Drain the chicken livers thoroughly in a strainer. Transfer to paper towels to dry. Look over the livers and remove anything unpleasant (like veins or blood; but don't go crazy). Season the livers well on both sides with salt and pepper. In the same cast-iron skillet, melt the 3 tablespoons butter in about 3 tablespoons olive oil over high heat. Add a small batch of the chicken livers, being sure not to overcrowd the pan, and cook until browned on both sides but still pink on the inside, about 5 minutes. Transfer the livers as they are cooked to the bowl with the onion mixture. Repeat to cook the remaining livers. Deglaze the pan between batches with sherry vinegar and pour the deglazing liquid over the livers in the bowl. Finally, when all of the livers are cooked, use the brandy to deglaze the pan and add it to the bowl with the rest. Let everything cool.

Once the livers and onions are cool, transfer them to a food processor. Put everything in at once and let the motor run—you want the mousse to be very smooth. Season with sherry vinegar, salt, and pepper as needed, tasting over and over again until you feel that it could not taste any better than it does. Transfer to a bowl, cover, and refrigerate. The mousse will hold well in the refrigerator for up to 1 week.

The Little Chef is the name of a chain of "motorway" restaurants in England. It is also the nickname Mark Firth gave to me when I first started working for him at Diner. This is my sandwich. Rebecca's is the Scuttlebutt, and Elizabeth's is the Clean Slate. To me, no sandwich menu would be complete without a salty, oily, cured-meat-and-cheese sandwich. This is an Italian-style sandwich featuring the beautiful pink, fat-studded pork product called mortadella.

You don't really *have* to make the green olive spread, as an approximation is surely available at the supermarket (unless you live in Ohio or Union City, NJ). But, as with everything, if you make it at home, you have the satisfaction of knowing you've done it—and probably done it better. This olive paste is extremely simple; it's nothing

The Little Chef

Mortadella, *pecorino toscano*, green olive spread, fresh parsley, olive oil

FOR THE GREEN OLIVE SPREAD

1 cup pitted Picholine olives

Extra-virgin olive oil as needed

1 sandwich-size piece of Focaccia (page 36)

2 tablespoons green olive spread

3 thin slices mortadella (we use Fra' Mani)

3 thin slices young *pecorino toscano*, preferably 30-day aged

6 leaves fresh parsley or basil

Extra-virgin olive oil for drizzling

MAKES 1 SANDWICH

but olives and oil. I recommend making a large batch and leaving it in the refrigerator to use as you like, when you like. Just make sure to cover the top with olive oil to prevent mold or spoilage. The recipe here makes enough for about eight sandwiches and will last, tightly covered in the refrigerator, for up to 1 month.

TO MAKE THE OLIVE SPREAD, put the olives in a food processor or a mortar. Process or pound with a pestle until the olives start to break down into small crumbly pieces. Add 1 tablespoon olive oil to loosen the mixture, then continue to process or pound, adding olive oil as necessary until a smooth paste forms.

Cut the focaccia in half horizontally and put on a plate, cut-sides up. Spread a generous layer of the olive spread evenly on the bottom half. Fold each slice of the mortadella in half and layer on top of the olive spread. Lay the cheese on top of the mortadella to cover, folding as needed to fit. Arrange the herb leaves on top of the cheese and drizzle everything with a little olive oil. Replace the top of the bread and press lightly to help hold the sandwich together. Serve right away.

Though all of us in the kitchen at Saltie eat meat, there is precious little room in our shop to store and prepare it, so there is very little of it on our menu. In the beginning, it was hard to undo the requisite thinking about meat. Not only have we all worked with it so much over the years, but we were also invested in one of the first revivals of the "whole animal" program in our locality. Our first week in business, we bought a two-hundred-pound pig from Flying Pigs Farm.

The Meat Hook

Pork loin, *romesco*, arugula, fried egg

1 sandwich-size piece of Focaccia (page 36)

3 tablespoons Romesco (page 52)

3 or 4 thin slices Brined Pork Roast (page 116)

1 small handful arugula

Extra-virgin olive oil

Sea salt

Juice of ½ lemon

1 large egg, cooked sunny (see page 63) (optional)

MAKES
1
SANDWICH

Upon receiving the pig, however, we immediately began to wonder what we were thinking. Meat had become an inseparable part of sustainability. But it struck us that if we just didn't overuse it on our menu, we wouldn't have to overinvest in a sustainable program that was too big for our needs.

That has turned out to be utterly liberating. Over time, we have come to rely on little things to bring some meatiness to the menu on a much smaller scale: chicken and chicken livers, smoked pork hocks, a brisket, ham. We are lucky to have two butcher shops in our neighborhood that supply us with meat that meets our standards without having to carry the weight, literally and figuratively, ourselves—the Meat Hook and Marlow & Daughters. This pork sandwich was developed with a leftover pork roast we had from a demo we did at the Meat Hook. So really this is a recipe for leftovers.

Cut the focaccia in half horizontally and put on a plate, cut-sides up. Spread the *romesco* evenly on the cut side of the bottom half. If your pork roast is just cooked, carve and place the slices on top of the *romesco*. Otherwise, reheat the sliced pork in a sauté pan over medium heat just until warmed through, then arrange on the bread.

In a small bowl, toss the arugula with a drizzle of olive oil, a pinch of sea salt, and the lemon juice and place on top of the pork. This may be enough for you, in which case, replace the top of the bread and serve. If you want to keep going, fry the egg and place it on top of the arugula. Then top with the bread and serve.

Brined Pork Roast

Just about every restaurant has a recipe for brined pork. In the days before heritage breeds were revived commonly and locally, one of the uses for brine was to make commercial pork more flavorful. We may not need to rely on it for the flavor we once did, but it remains a great preparation for just about any cut of pork.

4 cups water

¾ cup sugar

⅔ cup kosher salt, plus more for seasoning

3 to 4 pounds center-cut pork loin, bone off

12 fresh thyme sprigs

1 tablespoon coriander seeds

1 tablespoon fennel seeds

1 tablespoon whole black peppercorns

3 bay leaves

1 head garlic, cut in half

Freshly ground black pepper

**MAKES ENOUGH FOR
6 SANDWICHES**

Prepare a brine by pouring the water into a pot and stirring in the sugar and ⅔ cup salt. Bring to a boil over high heat and cook until the sugar and salt are dissolved. Remove from the heat and let cool. Place the pork loin in a large container and pour the brine over it. Add 3 quarts fresh water, then the thyme, spices, bay leaves, and garlic. Refrigerate the brined pork at least overnight or for up to 3 days.

Preheat the oven to 400°F.

Remove the pork from the brine and pat dry with paper towels. Season the pork well with salt and pepper. Heat a large cast-iron skillet over high heat. Add the pork and sear to brown on all sides, about 10 minutes total. When nicely browned, transfer to the oven and roast until firm and bouncy to the touch, 20 to 30 minutes, or until an instant-read thermometer inserted into the thickest part registers 140 to 145°F. Remove the pork from the oven and let rest for 5 minutes before carving into thin slices. Store any leftovers in an airtight container in the refrigerator for up to 3 days.

This is another character that we sort of killed off, but it continues to reappear in different forms from time to time. This sandwich is a classic French-style ham-and-cheese that is traditionally served on baguette. In the beginning, we served it on house-made Parker House rolls. But Elizabeth never liked Parker House rolls, and then Rebecca and I concurred . . . mostly because we had to get out of bed too early to make them and it made us grumpy. So we stopped producing the Gam.

We have since come to realize that the Gam is quite good on focaccia. Still, we haven't brought it back full time. Sometimes you just have to keep moving forward.

The Gam

Ham, Gruyère, curried pickled green tomatoes, herb butter

1 sandwich-size piece of Focaccia (page 36)

2 tablespoons Herb Butter (page 57)

4 thin slices Fra' Mani ham (see Note)

3 thin slices Gruyère

3 slices Curried Pickled Green Tomato (page 72)

MAKES 1 SANDWICH

Cut the focaccia in half horizontally and put on a plate, cut-sides up. Spread both cut sides with the herb butter. Layer the ham, cheese, and pickles on the bottom half of the bread, in that order. Replace the top of the bread and press lightly to help hold the sandwich together. Serve right away.

NOTE: We use a Fra' Mani product called "Little Ham," made by Paul Bertolli. We love its sweet, salty balance.

This very special sandwich was given its name by Dennis Spina, our collective soul mate and genius chef of the Roebling Tea Room (our local favorite and weekly book meeting locale). The Longshoreman had a very brief run on the Saltie menu. It turned out to be too much, too soon: We couldn't make enough meatballs to keep up with demand, and the sandwich collapsed under the weight of its own popularity.

We learned that if you have a meatball sandwich on the menu, only a vegetarian is going to order anything else. The Longshoreman threatened to capsize the boat. You can't stay afloat just selling out of one thing every day. As much as possible, there needs to be balance on the menu. This sandwich threw us off. And while I couldn't blame anyone for choosing it over others, it had to go. It was a strange and probably very stupid thing to do, killing off our most popular sandwich. Fortunately, we managed to survive. And the recipe survives for this book.

The components here also work great served as a platter. The meatballs are nicely accompanied by a salad of Farro, Peas, and Leeks (page 170).

The Longshoreman
Israeli meatballs, yogurt sauce, pickled vegetables, fresh herbs

3 Israeli Meatballs
(facing page)

1 piece Naan (page 40)

3 tablespoons Yogurt Sauce
(page 55)

1 tablespoon Pickled Beets
(page 73)

1 tablespoon Pickled Red
Onions (page 73)

2 tablespoons Fresh Herb Mix
(page 58)

Place the meatballs on the naan. Drizzle with the yogurt sauce and garnish with the pickled beets, red onions, and herbs. Serve right away.

MAKES 1 SANDWICH

Israeli Meatballs

The meatballs themselves (like the chicken liver mousse for the Balmy, see page 112) are the recipe of Nir Feller, a wonderful cook from Israel who worked at Diner until his visa ran out. Sadly, neither Nir nor his meatballs are my daily companions anymore. Nir returned to Israel, and I deeply miss his cooking—those meatballs, falafel, *imjadra* (a dish of lentils and bulgur), chilled radish soup, and a fantastic sandwich of potatoes and hard-boiled eggs that I can't quite remember or I'd steal that, too. He left us with a handful of gems.

This recipe makes enough meatballs for eight sandwiches. You can certainly divide the recipe, but it seems that when there are meatballs around, they always get eaten.

2 pounds ground beef

½ cup pistachios

½ cup dried cherries

1 teaspoon cumin seeds

½ cinnamon stick

4 whole allspice berries

1 arbol chile

1 small onion, minced

½ cup chopped fresh parsley

½ cup chopped fresh cilantro

2 large eggs, lightly beaten

Kosher salt

Freshly ground black pepper

Extra-virgin olive oil

MAKES 2 DOZEN MEATBALLS

Place the ground beef in a large bowl.

Chop the pistachios and cherries well and add to the bowl with the beef. Either in a mortar using a pestle or in a spice grinder, pound or grind the cumin, cinnamon, allspice, and chile to a fine powder and add to the bowl, along with the onion, parsley, cilantro, and eggs. Season generously with salt and pepper. Using your hands, mix well.

Drizzle a little olive oil into a cast-iron skillet and heat. Make one small meatball and place in the hot oil. Cook, turning as needed, until browned on all sides, about 5 minutes. Taste the tester meatball and correct the seasoning as necessary, then roll all of the meat mixture into golf ball–size balls.

Wipe out any burned bits from the skillet, add 1 tablespoon olive oil, and return to medium-high heat. Working in batches, add some of the meatballs, being careful not to overcrowd the pan. Cook, turning as needed to brown the meatballs evenly. By the time they are nicely browned, after 8 to 10 minutes, they should be properly cooked, just to medium. Transfer to paper towels to drain as they are finished. Store any leftover (!!) meatballs in an airtight container in the refrigerator for up to 1 week.

CHAPTER 3

BOWLS—SOUPS, EGG BOWLS, AND SALAD BOWLS

||||||||||||||||||||||||||||||||||||||||||||||||||||||||||||||||||||||||||||||||||||||||||||||||||||||||||||||||||

There have to be alternatives to sandwiches, not only for no-white-flour and gluten-free diets, but also because despite what I may have said at any other point in this book, you can't actually put everything you want to cook or eat between two squares of focaccia. While we may not *have* to do anything more than make sandwiches, we are still cooks who once in a while *want* to make something else.

Among the greatest joys of having a business like this are the regulars who rely on us to take care of them—daily, a few times a week, or only on weekends. These enthusiasts come in to see what else is available beyond the familiar sandwich menu. For them it's important that we offer more, and we have an obligation to keep them interested and well fed.

Salads and soups both complement and offer an alternative to sandwiches. We also always have an egg dish available, dubbed the "egg bowl" even when it comes on a plate. Our bowl dishes evolved from the fact that we all prefer to eat out of a bowl with (usually) a spoon. Is this because a bowl and spoon make it so much easier to scoop up every last bit? Is this because a spoon fits the mouth better than a fork does? Is it because a bowl in one hand and a spoon in the other is the best way to eat standing up, as we often do? Yes, yes, and yes.

||||||||||||||||||||||||||||||||||||||||||||||||||||||||||||||||||||||||||||||||||||||||||||||||||||||||||||||||||

There is also something deeply satisfying and generous about serving food in a bowl. This is somewhat contrary to the modern, and probably by now outdated, restaurant model in which I learned to cook—where salad and everything else was piled high on the plate, just to be toppled over in order to be consumed. Why would anyone prefer a salad that stood tall on a plate over one that was carefully contained within a bowl that could hold it steady? When I started making my own menus, I tried to serve anything I could in a bowl. The shape of the vessel itself contains a certain receptiveness, an openness, and an element of comfort. A bowl feels more like a gift. That, probably as much as anything else, explains the presence of these dishes on our menu.

Soups

I have a love-hate relationship with soup. I like to cook it, but I don't like to *serve* it. I rarely order it in a restaurant, yet there are soups that I would go out for. I like soup when it's apparent that the chef is inspired to make it, or if I am at a Vietnamese or Japanese restaurant. I love Italian soups—*ribollita*, minestrone, *brodo* with tortellini, escarole, and meatballs—but even these are everyday soups. Soups are not celebratory. They are workaday, sustaining. Perhaps that is what I both love and hate about them.

When I am inspired to make soup, I find it fully engaging and deeply satisfying. I like meals where everything is made in one pot, the layering of ingredients and flavors. Stirring and checking in. Witnessing the transformation from raw materials to simmering, aromatic, restorative meal. Plus I like anything served in a bowl.

We make soups at Saltie both as alternatives to a sandwich and to bring other seasonal ingredients to the menu. Soup also provides a great opportunity to make use of things we have left over in the kitchen: the ends of Gruyère or pecorino, extra chicken stock, a piece of ham, lots of bread. I think that is what soup is generally meant to be, a means to utilize and stretch what you have in the best possible way.

A version of this soup came from my greatest friend and mentor, Dave Wurth, who was the *chef de cuisine* at Savoy and one of the two most hilarious people I have ever known. I recall being introduced to this soup when I was working the salad station. Served chilled, it was the first soup I was ever responsible for. I distinctly remember the coriander seed and thinking, how wonderful and odd. This is not quite the same recipe—Dave's would be more complex. He always added a little something extra, a twist on the classic approach. I could never understand how he arrived there. I followed his logic to a point, and then he always surprised me.

Chilled Cucumber Soup with Yogurt and Coriander

4 large slicing cucumbers

2 tablespoons coriander seeds, lightly toasted and pounded with a mortar and pestle

Sea salt

1 cup water

2 cups yogurt, homemade (see page 54) or best-quality store-bought

½ cup chopped fresh mint

This is a quick, cooling soup, good for when it's too hot out to eat. It's almost a beverage and can be treated as such. We also like to garnish it with some sliced radish.

Peel and seed the cucumbers and cut them into 1-inch pieces.

Place the cucumbers, coriander seeds, and a good pinch of salt in a blender or a food processor and pulse to a coarse purée. Add water and process until smooth. Transfer the cucumber purée to a bowl and whisk in the yogurt and mint. Season with more salt, if needed. Refrigerate until well chilled, about 2 hours. Whisk again before serving. Ladle into bowls and serve cold.

This soup is about nettles and ramps. Potatoes give the greens body and bulk and provide a velvety, flavorful, yet fairly neutral base for their qualities to shine.

Potato, Nettle, Ramp, and Pecorino Soup

6 medium Yukon gold potatoes

12 large ramps, well washed and trimmed

3 tablespoons unsalted butter

3 tablespoons extra-virgin olive oil

Sea salt

One ½-inch-by-3-inch end piece of *pecorino toscano*, plus shavings for garnish

Chicken stock as needed (about 4 cups)

1 cup Nettle Sauce (page 49)

Freshly ground black pepper

MAKES 4 SERVINGS

Peel the potatoes and cut them in half lengthwise. Lay them cut-side down on a cutting board and cut them in half again lengthwise, then crosswise into ¼-inch slices. Set aside.

Cut the ramps to separate the white parts from the green. Cut the white parts into ¼-inch slices. Stack the ramp greens and slice them thinly into a chiffonade.

In a soup pot, melt the butter in the olive oil over medium heat. When the butter begins to sizzle, add the ramp whites and a pinch of salt and sauté until soft, about 3 minutes. Add the potatoes and pecorino to the ramps along with another pinch of salt and give everything a good stir. Cook the potatoes for a few minutes to get them going and then add enough chicken stock just to cover the potatoes. Bring to a simmer, then reduce the heat to low heat and cook gently until the potatoes are falling-apart soft, 20 to 30 minutes longer.

At this point, stir in the nettle sauce and the ramp greens and cook just until heated through. Ladle the soup into bowls and top with an additional shaving of pecorino, a drizzle of olive oil, and a crack of pepper. Serve hot.

As hard as it is to face the waning of tomato season, there is comfort in roasting them for a few final weeks before saying goodbye. Treated as such, they can be added to just about anything or served as a side dish. This soup is a good transitional meal between summer and fall. Not too much of a shock to the system, it is a hot soup, but one that still holds the flavors of summer.

Fregola is a little, round, toasted pasta. It's dense and chewy and perfect for adding to soup. If you can't find it you could substitute a grain like *farro*, wheat berries, bulgur, or couscous.

Late-Summer Roasted Tomato Soup with Fregola and Kale

12 Roma (plum) tomatoes

Extra-virgin olive oil

Sea salt

2 cups *fregola* (see recipe introduction)

12 large garlic cloves, sliced

6 fresh rosemary sprigs

6 fresh sage sprigs

1 bunch Tuscan or purple kale, tough stems and spines removed, roughly chopped

MAKES 4 SERVINGS

Preheat the oven to 400°F.

Core the tomatoes and cut in half lengthwise. Place the tomatoes, skin-side down, on a baking sheet. Drizzle them evenly with olive oil and season with sea salt. Roast until they lose their water, char a little, and become concentrated, about 30 minutes.

Meanwhile, cook the *fregola* as you would any dried pasta, in a pot of well-salted boiling water. When the *fregola* is al dente, about 10 minutes, drain it through a colander and toss with a little olive oil to keep it from sticking together.

In a heavy-bottomed soup pot, heat 3 tablespoons olive oil over medium heat. Add the garlic and cook until it turns golden, about 3 minutes. Add the rosemary and sage to the garlic and oil. Allow the herbs to sizzle, then stir in the tomatoes. Add 4 cups water, stir to mix, and let everything warm to a simmer.

Add the kale and a good pinch of salt to the pot, return to a simmer, and cook until the kale is very tender, about 10 minutes. Add the cooked *fregola* and warm through. Ladle into bowls, top with a drizzle of olive oil and a sprinkle of sea salt, and serve hot.

This is kind of a fancy version of broccoli and Cheddar soup. We often have the ends of cheese left from the sandwich preparations. I have learned in the course of making soup at Saltie that cheese and chicken stock make a very delicious soup base for vegetables. When it comes to simple vegetable soups like this, I think that less is more; allowing one or two ingredients to come together makes for a more thorough exploration of what the vegetable is.

Cauliflower, Leek, and Gruyère Soup

3 tablespoons unsalted butter

3 tablespoons extra-virgin olive oil

4 leeks, white and tender green parts, thinly sliced on the diagonal (bias)

Kosher salt

1 head cauliflower, cut into small florets

1 chunk Gruyère, about 4 inches wide and 1 inch thick

Chicken stock, as needed (about 4 cups)

1 cup fresh parsley

MAKES 4 SERVINGS

In a soup pot over medium-high heat, melt the butter in the olive oil. When the butter begins to sizzle, add the leeks and a pinch of salt. Sauté the leeks until they begin to wilt, about 5 minutes. Add the cauliflower and another pinch of salt and cook the cauliflower and leeks until they begin to come together, about 3 minutes longer.

Add the hunk of Gruyère and give everything a good stir. Add just enough chicken stock to cover the vegetables. Turn the heat down to low and simmer until the cauliflower is tender, 20 to 30 minutes. At this point the cheese will have mostly melted. Taste and adjust the seasoning, stir in the parsley, and serve hot.

Here's another big soup.

Rebecca is always craving a kind of satisfying heat that eludes her. New York doesn't have the Indian curries that she misses from home. As a result, she goes through periods of trying to make her own curry, taking over the kitchen with every spice on the shelf. She makes this soup a lot, and each time it's a little different. When it's just right, it's the best possible thing to eat.

There are three varieties of squash I particularly recommend here for their dense, earthy, vegetal qualities, but a butternut will certainly work just fine, too.

Curried Squash and Red Lentil Soup

1 smallish kuri, kabocha, or Hubbard squash

3 tablespoons extra-virgin olive oil, plus ½ cup or as needed

Kosher salt

1 tablespoon whole cardamom pods

2 teaspoons coriander seeds

1 teaspoon cumin seeds

1 teaspoon fenugreek seeds

1 teaspoon whole black peppercorns

2 pasilla or ancho chiles

2 arbol chiles

2 medium Spanish onions, quartered

6 large garlic cloves, peeled but left whole

One 1-inch piece fresh ginger, peeled

Preheat the oven to 400°F.

Using a large, sharp knife, cut the squash in half. Scrape out and discard the seeds. Peel the squash with a vegetable peeler, then cut the flesh into 1-inch cubes. Put the squash on a heavy-duty baking sheet or in a large roasting pan. Drizzle in the 3 tablespoons olive oil, sprinkle with salt, and toss to mix well and coat. Spread the squash in a single layer and roast until tender, about 20 minutes.

Meanwhile, in a small, dry skillet over medium heat, toast the cardamom, stirring, until lightly browned and aromatic, about 2 minutes. Remove from the heat and transfer to a mortar. Let cool slightly, pound the cardamom to loosen the pod, then remove the pods and discard them. (If you don't have a mortar, use a knife to help you crack off the cardamom pods on a cutting board and use a spice grinder for all of the following grinding.) Return the skillet to medium heat and add the coriander, cumin, fenugreek, and peppercorns. Toast, stirring constantly, until fragrant, about 2 minutes. Transfer to the mortar. Toast the chiles in the skillet until they puff and release their fragrance, about 3 minutes. Remove from the heat and set aside until cool enough to handle. Slit the chiles

½ cinnamon stick

1 tablespoon ground turmeric

1 teaspoon cayenne pepper

1 pound red lentils, picked over
for grit and stones and rinsed

Juice of ½ lemon

Toasted sesame seeds
for garnish

Yogurt Sauce (page 55)
for serving

and discard most of the seeds, then add them to the mortar with the spices. Using a pestle (or in a spice grinder), pound all the toasted spices and chiles until coarsely ground.

In a blender, combine the onions, garlic, ginger, and 1 cup water and process to a smooth purée. Place a large soup pot on the stove and pour in the ½ cup olive oil. It should cover the entire bottom of the pot; add more if necessary. Place over high heat, add the puréed onion mixture, and sprinkle generously with salt. Cook, stirring often, until all of the water evaporates, about 10 minutes, and then add the ground spices and chiles. Cook until the onion begins to get a little color, about 5 minutes. If at any point the onion mixture begins to get too dry and stick, add a little more olive oil. Add the cinnamon stick, turmeric, and cayenne. Stir to mix everything together. Add the lentils and stir well to coat with oil and spices. Add enough water to cover the lentils by 1 inch and another pinch or two of salt and stir again, then lower the heat to medium-low.

When the lentils are mostly cooked, after about 30 minutes, add the squash to the pot along with just enough water to cover everything. Simmer together until the lentils are cooked through, about 10 minutes longer. Taste for salt and adjust. Add a squeeze of lemon to brighten the flavors.

Ladle into bowls, sprinkle the toasted sesame seeds on top, and serve hot with the yogurt sauce.

I started cooking with other cuts of meat like this when we opened Marlow & Daughters butcher shop in an effort to become more knowledgeable about how to use them at home. These cuts of meat are really exceptional; they may take a little coaxing but have great flavor and nutritional value and provide the opportunity to taste beef in a way that isn't just about a steak or a hamburger. I like serving meat in this way, as a small flavor-building element rather than a big hunk on a plate. It's also economical—a little goes a long way. Beef shin in particular gives a great beefy essence to this soup.

Be patient and leave yourself plenty of time to make this soup—the beef shank will take many hours to cook.

Beef Shin and Farro Soup

1 meaty, 3- to 4-inch crosscut beef shank

Sea salt and freshly ground black pepper

3 tablespoons extra-virgin olive oil, plus more for drizzling

3 carrots

2 leeks

¼ cup fresh parsley leaves, stems reserved

1 cup *farro*

4 red radishes, thinly sliced

4 scallions, thinly sliced

MAKES 2 SERVINGS

Season the beef shank well with salt and pepper and let it sit for at least 1 hour at room temperature or up to overnight, covered in the refrigerator, if you have the time and foresight.

In a heavy-bottomed soup pot over medium-high heat, heat the 3 tablespoons olive oil. Add the beef shank and sear until nicely browned on all sides, about 15 minutes total. Remove it from the pot, discard the oil, and return the shank to the pot. Add enough water to reach about two-thirds of the way up the sides of the shank. Cut 1 carrot and 1 whole leek in half lengthwise and add to the pot, along with the stems from the parsley. Cover the pot, bring to a simmer, and cook the beef shank until tender, about 4 hours. Check on it periodically, adding water as necessary if it gets too low. Once the beef shank is cooked, you can hold it in the refrigerator and make the soup the next day.

CONTINUED

Otherwise, toward the end of the cooking time, bring a saucepan three-quarters full of well-salted water to a boil. Add the *farro* and cook until tender, about 10 minutes. Drain the *farro* and toss with a little olive oil. Set aside. Slice the remaining 2 carrots and 1 leek thinly on the diagonal (bias).

When the meat is tender, remove from the heat and let cool slightly, then remove the meat from the bone and pull or slice it into bite-size pieces. Put the meat back in the broth and add the sliced carrots, leeks, and radishes. Place over medium-low heat and simmer until the vegetables are cooked through, about 10 minutes. Taste and season the broth with salt. Add the *farro* and scallions and cook just to warm through. Ladle the soup into bowls and garnish with the parsley leaves and a grind of black pepper. Serve hot.

This recipe demonstrates our general approach to soup making. It's mostly vegetable, given a big, smoky depth of flavor by the pork hock, and thickened with leftover bread. This soup is also delicious with a little *pimentón* added at the end.

Cabbage, Celery Root, Smoked Pork Hock, and Bread Soup

1 smoked pork hock

3 tablespoons extra-virgin olive oil, plus more for drizzling

1 large yellow onion, thinly sliced lengthwise

Sea salt

2 celery roots, peeled and cut into ½-inch dice

1 small head green or savoy cabbage, thinly sliced

Leaves of 12 sprigs thyme

2 cups diced day-old Focaccia (page 36) or other crusty bread

Leaves of 1 small bunch fresh parsley

Freshly ground black pepper

Place the pork hock in a medium soup pot over medium-high heat. Add just enough water to reach the top of the hock. Bring to a boil, reduce heat to low, and simmer for 1 hour.

In a separate, larger pot, heat the 3 tablespoons olive oil over medium-high heat. Add the onion and a good pinch of sea salt and sauté until the onion begins to turn golden, about 5 minutes. Add the celery root and another pinch of salt and sauté with the onion for a few minutes. Add the cabbage and another pinch of salt, mix everything well, reduce the heat to medium, and cook until everything starts to come together, about 5 minutes. Lower the heat a little more and add the pork hock and its cooking liquid. Stir in the thyme and simmer the soup until the celery root is tender, about 20 minutes longer.

Add the bread cubes to the soup a little at a time, enough to give it body but not so much that it takes over. (You do not want a mass of wet bread.) Mix the bread in well and let it soak up some liquid and warm through, but don't leave it so long that it becomes bloated. Stir the parsley into the soup and ladle into individual bowls. Drizzle each with olive oil, garnish with a pinch of sea salt and a crack of pepper, and serve hot.

Here's a soup that can make enduring the New York winter worthwhile and provide a day's worth of entertainment. Ribollita is hearty stewlike dish that is comforting and satisfying. It's practically in another class altogether, just barely still a soup and moving toward something else. The addition of bread to the beans makes it dense and chewy, something to sink your teeth into. Ribollita satisfies the same thing in me that a bowl of pasta does. Which is saying a lot.

Ribollita means "reboiled," and is traditionally a soup that is made a day ahead and then reheated (or even baked) the next day, with bread to stretch it. This recipe is nudged toward being able to cook and eat in the same day, but there will be leftovers to reheat the next day, and you will see how the flavors change.

This recipe is for a big batch of soup.

Ribollita

FOR THE BEANS

1 pound dried cranberry, borlotti, or cannellini beans

1 small bunch fresh thyme

1 small bunch fresh sage

6 bay leaves

1 head garlic

¼ cup extra-virgin olive oil

Kosher salt

TO MAKE THE BEANS, pick them over for grit and stones. Place them in a large bowl, add plenty of water, and let soak overnight. Drain and rinse the beans in a colander, then transfer to a large pot. Add 12 cups fresh water and bring to a boil over high heat, skimming with a ladle any foam that rises to the surface.

Tie the thyme and sage together with kitchen string and add to the pot along with the bay leaves. Peel the head of garlic, slice the cloves in half lengthwise, and add to the beans. Add the olive oil, reduce the heat to low, and simmer until the beans are tender, 1 hour. *Really* cook these beans at a simmer. You don't want them banging together as they cook; you more want them floating around. The cooking time will vary based on how long the beans soaked and their general freshness.

Once the beans start to swell, begin tasting them, and when they taste exactly as you would want them to be if you were going to eat them right then, add a pinch or two of kosher salt and then cook them a little longer (see Note).

At this point, you can store the beans in their liquid in an airtight container in the refrigerator for up to 3 days.

FOR THE SOUP

½ cup extra-virgin olive oil, plus more as needed

2 medium Spanish onions, diced

8 large garlic cloves, sliced

Sea salt

2 large carrots, peeled and diced

6 ribs celery, diced

1 bunch fresh parsley, roughly chopped

Two 28-ounce cans whole plum tomatoes

1 small head savoy cabbage, cored and thinly sliced (about 4 cups)

1 bunch *cavolo nero* (black) or Tuscan kale, thinly sliced

6 cups cubed Focaccia (page 36) or other crusty bread

MAKES 8-10 SERVINGS

TO MAKE THE SOUP, heat the ½ cup olive oil in a large enamel-coated cast-iron pot over high heat. Add the onions and garlic and a good sprinkle of sea salt and sauté until the onions begin to release their liquid, about 5 minutes. Add the carrots and celery along with another sprinkle of sea salt, reduce the heat to medium, and continue to sauté. If at any point the mixture starts to look dry, add a little more olive oil; it should be moving around in the pot very well. Stir the vegetables regularly to prevent them from sticking to the pot or cooking unevenly. After about 20 minutes, when the vegetables have softened a bit and are starting to come together, maybe even turned a little golden, add the parsley and cook for 5 minutes longer.

Crush the canned tomatoes into the pot with your hands, then add the juice from the cans. Stir in more salt if needed, reduce the heat to low, and simmer the vegetable mixture, stirring often, until the tomatoes lose their tinniness, about 30 minutes.

Add the cabbage and kale to the pot. Add 2 cups water and stir well. Taste and adjust the seasoning. Cook until the cabbage is wilted, 20 to 30 minutes.

Drain the cooked beans and add to the soup. Add 4 cups water and stir well. Turn the heat as low as you can and simmer for about 2 hours, being careful to stir and scrape the bottom of the pot occasionally to make sure that the beans are not sticking. The longer you can cook the ribollita at this point, the deeper the flavor will become. One thing is certain—you want to cook out the red color of the tomatoes and the bright green of the cabbage and kale. The soup will begin to take on an overall rust color. That's when you'll know it is done.

When you think the soup is about done, taste and adjust the seasoning again. Understand that this soup will seem to need a lot of salt. Don't feel uncomfortable

CONTINUED

about that, as what you are essentially cooking are vegetables and water. When the ribollita is cooked, add the focaccia and stir it around well so it absorbs the liquid and begins to fall apart, 5 to 10 minutes. Ladle into bowls, drizzle with a little extra-virgin olive oil and a pinch of sea salt, and serve hot.

NOTE: The salt makes the beans harden up a little again, so if you salt them and then take them right off the heat, they will be less cooked than when you originally tasted them. You must account for this effect in the cooking process when seasoning. This is also why you don't add salt to beans as they cook—it will cause them to harden and take much longer to cook.

Lake Superior

Cock-a-Leekie is an old Scottish recipe for soup composed of chicken, leeks, and prunes. As with many good old recipes from the United Kingdom, it has a name that's just a little funny, and here in America sometimes it feels like our customers think we're being naughty, trying to make them say things that they might feel uncomfortable about. I assure you one and all, we're really not that clever. We just know how to pick a recipe that suits our sensibility, and this one does on all levels.

Cock-a-Leekie

I would put this soup in the worthy-of-a-trip-on-its-own category. It's quite special. I've really never had anything else like it. Given that there are so few ingredients, it is essential that you use the best-quality chicken you can get. That will make all the difference in the final result. The chicken should be velvety and the stock rich, with a good layer of fat on top (which I like to keep a little of in the soup). The prunes provide an element of sweetness but more lend themselves to enriching the stock, almost making it beefy. The leeks balance everything out, bringing some sharpness.

This is a very simple recipe, stolen from Fergus Henderson. It may seem confusing or unclear because the procedure is unusual. Don't panic. All you need to understand going in is that you are simultaneously cooking the chicken and making stock, and then you make a stock again with the chicken bones.

CONTINUED

One 3- to 4-pound chicken

2 large leeks

Kosher salt

3 tablespoons extra-virgin
olive oil

½ cup prunes

Freshly ground black pepper

Focaccia (page 36) for serving

Place the chicken in a stockpot and add just enough water to cover it. Remove the dark green tops of the leeks and rinse well. Add the leek tops and a good handful of salt to the chicken pot. Place over medium-high heat and bring the water to a boil. As soon as it boils, turn the heat off and let the chicken cool completely in its cooking liquid, about an hour. When cool, remove the chicken from the cooking liquid—which is now stock. Remove and discard the skin and pull the meat off the bones. Try to leave the meat in large, generous pieces, rather than shredding it. Put the meat in a bowl, cover, and refrigerate until you're ready to assemble the final soup. Strain the stock, return it to the pot, and add the chicken bones. Simmer for 1 hour, to extract even more flavor out of the bones. Strain the stock into a bowl and discard the bones. Wipe the pot clean.

Thinly slice the white and light-green parts of the leeks on the diagonal (bias). Soak the cut leeks in plenty of water to release any grit. Lift the leeks out of the water and transfer to a strainer to drain. Heat the olive oil in the soup pot over medium-high heat. Add the leeks, season with salt, and sauté until they begin to wilt, about 5 minutes, then add enough chicken stock to cover the leeks by 1 inch. Stir in the prunes, reduce the heat to low, and simmer until the prunes plump up, about 10 minutes. Add the chicken meat and the remainder of the stock, season the whole pot with salt, and simmer, still on low, until everything just comes together, about 20 minutes. The prunes should give the stock a deep brown color and a nice sweetness.

Ladle into bowls and crack black pepper on top. Serve hot with the focaccia.

Egg Bowls

I've been a little obsessed with the Rolling Stones for the past year or so. I realize that I am a little late to the game with this one, having spent most of youth focused on Led Zeppelin as my greatest love; but here I am, and, despite my embarrassment or self-consciousness, I find myself referring to them in the course of many conversations. Particularly Keith. I've never imagined that my rock heroes think much about food, and I never expected to find anything relevant to writing this book while reading Keith Richards' autobiography. But there it was—a passage where he talks about recording in the south of France, working all night and then taking his speedboat to Italy for breakfast. And the reason why? Keith: "We liked the way the Italians cooked their eggs, and the bread." I would be happy to be on the receiving end of that sentiment by anyone, if not Keith Richards.

I can't imagine writing this book without a pause to praise the egg. The egg is what gives substance to Saltie. It is our essential protein. Without it, we would just be serving salad on bread. Whether it is the element that binds the potato tortilla, the means to emulsifying mayonnaise, the luxuriousness that is the soft scramble, or the clean and direct added value that is the hard boil, the egg is our muscle, our workhorse. Everything that I like to eat, I like to eat better with an egg on it—salad, grains, beans, toast.

CONTINUED

I never thought that eighteen years into my culinary career I would become so enamored of eggs. There were so many things I fell in love with along the way. First cabbage and beets and all of the new vegetables I had never really eaten. For a long, long time, pork. Braising cuts of beef. Bluefish, bass, branzino, sardines, anchovies, clams, and oysters. Ramps, radishes, bitter greens, artichokes, herbs, fresh shell beans. Always tomatoes, eggplant, and peppers. But eggs! What a surprise. Like marrying the high school nerd long into middle age. I had no idea that the egg had been waiting for me to notice it and to fall in love.

Eggs are quick and easy to cook but require attention and technique. One shouldn't take their simplicity as a pass to be careless. There are rigorous techniques that govern egg cookery, each style requiring an entirely different approach. Though one might seem to lead to the other, to fry an egg sunny-side up is quite different than to prepare it over easy. The specificity of times and stages between a soft and hard boil; the condemnation of a mere speck of brown on an egg coming out of a French kitchen; whether to use whole butter, clarified butter, or olive oil . . . things like this and many others must be considered when setting out to prepare this confection—which in most cases takes mere minutes.

And then there's the omelet. In the professional sphere, the measure of one's culinary talents is often determined by whether or not one can make a perfect omelet (to which anyone who has sought to become an instructor at a French cooking school will attest). Given that you can find an egg prepared just about anywhere, it is easy to think of them as nothing special. They may seem cheap and easy. But observe them more closely and find that they are so much more than that. Inexpensive perhaps, but utterly unparalleled.

Initially, the "egg bowl" was what we made for ourselves for breakfast—something light enough to be able to carry on working but (unlike the impulsive corner of focaccia smeared with ricotta) something that might actually provide some real sustenance and nutritional value. As is often the case with the food you make for each other as a staff meal, you realize that it should go on the menu, and so the egg bowl was released to the public.

"Papi" is one of Rebecca's monikers. As she loves all things Spanish flavored, and *papi* is near to *papas*—potatoes—this seemed an appropriate title for this dish made with *romesco*, a rich, dense, smoky, spicy sauce. It particularly lends itself to vegetables, providing richness from the nuts and olive oil.

Papi Romesco
Soft-scrambled eggs, potatoes, peppers, *romesco*

8 medium Yukon gold or other waxy potatoes (about 2 pounds total weight), peeled

Extra-virgin olive oil

Kosher salt

3 large red bell peppers or Italian frying peppers

1 cup Romesco (page 52)

8 large eggs

Sea salt

Preheat the oven to 350°F.

Cut the potatoes in half and then cut them into wedges. On a heavy-duty baking sheet or in a large roasting pan, toss the potatoes with olive oil and a generous sprinkling of salt. Spread in a single layer and roast until golden brown on the edges, about 30 minutes.

Meanwhile, cut the tops off the bell peppers and then cut them in half lengthwise. Remove the seeds and cut into ½-inch strips. In a cast-iron skillet over high heat, heat 3 tablespoons olive oil. Working in batches if necessary, add the bell peppers and spread in a single layer. Season the peppers with salt and cook them until they brown, and even char, turning them once with a pair of tongs. Add additional oil to the pan if it starts to get too dry. Continue on this way until all of the peppers are cooked.

When the potatoes are done, toss them with the peppers in a large bowl and then portion into four individual bowls. Distribute 2 tablespoons of *romesco* about and around the top of the potato and pepper mixture. Soft-scramble the eggs (see page 62) and spoon them on top of the potatoes. Sprinkle everything with sea salt and drizzle with olive oil. Serve right away, with extra *romesco* on the side.

This is barely a recipe. It's a way to use up leftover rice. But it's one of my all-time favorite things to eat for breakfast or lunch. It includes everything I want—grains, eggs, scallions, and sesame seeds. Yogurt sauce and hot sauce are also welcome here.

Fried Rice with Scallions and Sesame Seeds

2 tablespoons extra-virgin olive oil

2 garlic cloves, thinly sliced

1 cup leftover steamed rice (or other grain)

1 large egg

Sea salt

3 scallions, thinly sliced

1 teaspoon toasted sesame seeds

MAKES 1 SERVING

Heat the olive oil in a nonstick skillet over medium-high heat. Add the garlic and sauté until it begins to sizzle and turn golden, about 1 minute. Add the rice and sauté until warmed through. Crack an egg into the center of the rice. Season just the egg with sea salt.

Turn the heat to low and stir the egg into the rice—it will mostly cook in the residual heat of the rice. Be careful not to overcook the egg; ideally it will be just a little runny when you eat it. Toss in the scallions and transfer to an individual bowl. Sprinkle with the sesame seeds and serve with a spoon.

While succotash is traditionally a dish of corn and lima beans, I have come to see succotash as a mix of vegetables at their seasonal peak, cooked with a little cream. Therefore, the first bowl of succotash is, to me, one of the great triumphs of spring. Finally there are enough vegetables to really make something—a mixed dish of something. This recipe can be altered depending on what's available. Early in the season it may be composed of ramps and greens; later asparagus, fava beans, and English peas; in the late summer, shell beans.

Because we are not a traditional restaurant, it seems that we must either serve everything on focaccia or in a bowl with an egg on it. While succotash is quite wonderful with an egg on it, it can also be eaten without an egg, a nice complement to fish or lamb.

Succotash

Snap peas, radish, spring onion, butter lettuce, fresh chives, cream, poached egg

1 cup sugar snap peas

1 cup shelled English peas or fava beans

¼ cup extra-virgin olive oil

1 cup thinly sliced spring onions

Sea salt

8 red globe radishes, quartered

¼ cup heavy cream

1 small bunch fresh chives, minced

White wine vinegar

4 large eggs

1 head butter lettuce, leaves washed and separated

Freshly ground pepper

Bring a large saucepan three-quarters full of water to a boil. Have ready a large bowl of ice water.

With a paring knife, trim the stem ends of the snap peas and pull the strings off the pods on both sides. Cut into ½-inch slices on the diagonal (bias). Add the snap peas and English peas to the boiling water and blanch for 1 minute. Drain, plunge into the ice bath to stop the cooking, and drain again. Set aside in a strainer to drain completely.

In a large skillet or sauté pan over medium-high heat, heat the olive oil. Add the spring onions and a pinch of salt and cook until the onion begins to wilt, about 3 minutes. Add the radishes and season again with salt. Sauté the radishes with the spring onions until they start to soften. Proceed carefully—you want to retain the vitality of the vegetable, so cook the radishes just until tender, about 3 minutes. Add the snap peas and English peas and stir to warm through. Add the cream and simmer until reduced to a nice thickened sauce, about 3 minutes. Toss in the chives and check the seasoning again.

MAKES 4 SERVINGS

Meanwhile, bring a small pot of water to a low boil. Add a pinch of salt and a capful of white wine vinegar. Crack the eggs into a ladle one at a time and lower them into the simmering water. If the heat goes down below an active simmer once all of the eggs are in, turn it up. Cook until the whites are fully set and each yolk is holding its own. One at a time, lift the eggs out of the water with a slotted spoon, shaking gently to remove excess water.

Place a few leaves of butter lettuce in each of four individual bowls. Spoon the succotash over the lettuce. Grind a little pepper on top of the succotash. Place an egg on top of each bowl of succotash and serve right away.

We started making this dish at Marlow under Rebecca's insistence. At the time we didn't have a proper kitchen, so we needed to make things that could be served cold or at room temperature. This dish perfectly solved the problem of how to make something for lunch that is substantive yet does not require any heat in the moment.

Kedgeree
Curried rice, smoked whitefish, hard-boiled egg, yogurt sauce

2 cups white basmati rice

¼ cup extra-virgin olive oil

1 large yellow onion, finely chopped

4 garlic cloves, thinly sliced

Kosher salt

3 tablespoons curry powder

1½ cups milk

One 2-pound smoked whitefish

4 hard-boiled eggs (see page 64), quartered

1 cup Yogurt Sauce (page 55)

4 scallions, thinly sliced

MAKES 4 SERVINGS

Rinse the rice, then soak in a bowl of fresh cold water for 30 minutes. Drain through a strainer. Place a heavy-bottomed pot with a tight-fitting lid over medium-high heat and add the olive oil. When the olive oil is hot but not smoking, add the onion and garlic and sprinkle with salt. Cook, stirring, until the onion begins to turn golden, about 5 minutes. Add the curry powder and sauté with the onion for 1 minute. Add the rice and stir to coat well with the oil, curry, and onion. If the mixture seems too dry at this point, add a little more olive oil.

Add the milk and 1½ cups water to the pot and stir the rice well. Taste the liquid for salt, adding more if necessary. Bring the rice to just nearly a boil, put the lid on, and lower the heat to a gentle simmer. Cook until all the liquid is absorbed, about 15 minutes. Turn off the heat and let the rice steam a little more, then let it cool a little, 5 to 10 minutes longer.

Meanwhile, place the fish down flat on a cutting board and remove the skin. You will see a line of pin bones running down the center of the fillet. Using a paring knife or your hands, carefully remove the fish from either side of the pin bones. Once the top fillet has been removed, pull up the tail of the fish and detach the fish frame from the bottom fillet. Flake the bottom fillet from the pin bones and skin. Go over the whitefish again, being careful to remove as many bones as possible— although it's pretty impossible to get them all.

Portion the rice into four individual bowls. Place a serving of whitefish on top of the rice and the sliced hard-boiled egg on top of the fish. Add a generous amount of the yogurt sauce, top with the scallions, and serve right away.

Salad Bowls

The salad station has always been my favorite station to work in the professional kitchen. The common contemporary American description of the salad station is the entry-level position for kids out of cooking school or the place where the pokey ones who'll never make it to the hot line get stuck. Understood in this way, the salad station can be a career beginner and ender all in one. If you graduate from it you can move on to other stations in the kitchen, and if you don't there's nowhere else for you to go.

I have always been of the opinion that the salad station—which generally means all of the starters on a menu—is grossly undervalued. I like to think of this station in the classical sense, as the *garde manger*, the keeper of the food. In this incarnation the person who works the station is the one who makes sure the lettuce isn't being manhandled, the herbs aren't wet or bruised, the eggs are perfectly boiled, the vinaigrette and mayonnaise are delicious: the one who knows what needs to be used first and keeps the refrigerator clean and organized. This is the salad station that I like to work. And this is how I think of Saltie, as a big salad station. We are the *Garde Mangers*.

CONTINUED

And then there's salad, the leafy dish, not the station. I could not happily survive without a healthy allotment of salad greens. There is nothing like the leafiness, lightness, roughage, and jolt of vitamins a salad provides, instantly putting one back in balance. Every year when the first spring greens arrive, I am reminded of how perfectly the season gives you what you need just when you need it. Salad greens are nature's reward for a long and hefty winter.

Further along there is salad that is anything that can be put in a bowl and tossed with olive oil and vinegar or lemon juice. This could include grains, vegetables, eggs, meat, or fish. They're a salad, too.

I was handed a plate of raw shredded carrots at a bar in Ferrier Larçon, a tiny village of cave dwellers in the Loire Valley, and instantly fell for *salade rapide*—a fast, thoughtless salad. It seems like a French joke, raw shredded vegetables with a little vinaigrette, maybe.

I like a salad like this in the dead of winter when there's nothing left to eat. It provides a little vibrancy. It can also be diluted by mixing it with some lettuce or made even richer with the addition of feta cheese. We dress it up with a little pistachio and parsley. You can use other root vegetables in this salad, like celery root or turnips. It's also great tossed with a little of our all-purpose Yogurt Sauce (page 55) in addition to the vinaigrette.

Salade Rapide

½ cup pistachios

Extra-virgin olive oil
for drizzling

Sea salt

2 medium carrots, peeled

2 medium beets, peeled

¼ cup Lazy Housewife
Vinaigrette (page 48)

¼ cup chopped fresh parsley

MAKES 4 SERVINGS

Preheat the oven to 350°F. Put the pistachios on a baking sheet or in a small baking dish, drizzle with olive oil, sprinkle with salt, and toss to coat. Roast until they turn bright green, about 3 minutes. Let cool and chop coarsely.

With either a mandolin or a Swiss vegetable peeler, slice the carrots and beets into thin slices. Place the carrots and beets in a bowl and toss with the vinaigrette. Let them sit for 10 minutes to macerate. Add the pistachios and parsley and toss to mix. Season with salt and serve right away.

People either love or hate eggplant. I'm sure by now you can imagine which side of the equation I am on.

This is a dip, a relish, or a salad, which means it can be eaten on its own or served as an accompaniment to something else, like lamb or grilled meat, or as part of an appetizer plate. It's also completely delicious on the Clean Slate (page 84). I have really come to prefer cooking eggplant in this way. It's clean and easy, doesn't require sautéing in a lot of oil, and the natural creaminess of the vegetable comes through. I call for white eggplant here because I find it to be much less bitter and itchy than black. Grill it if you can; the smoke is perfect with this dish.

Eggplant Salad with Sesame Seeds

2 large firm eggplants, preferably white (about 2 pounds total weight)

Extra-virgin olive oil

6 garlic cloves, sliced

Sea salt

Juice of 1 to 2 lemons

¼ cup chopped fresh parsley

2 tablespoons toasted sesame seeds

MAKES 4 SERVINGS

Build a hot fire in a charcoal grill or preheat the oven to 400°F.

Leave the skin on the eggplants and rub them with olive oil. If cooking in the oven, put the eggplants on a baking sheet. Whether grilling or roasting, cook the eggplants until they collapse and get very soft, turning them as they go. It should take about 15 minutes on a hot fire or 20 minutes in the oven. Let cool.

When the eggplants are cool enough to handle, peel off the skins. The eggplant will be quite soft, but still chop the flesh well so that it's almost like a purée. Sizzle the garlic in a pan with a little olive oil over medium heat until golden. Place the eggplant in a bowl and pour the garlic and oil over it. Season the eggplant with more olive oil, sea salt, and lemon juice. Serve garnished with the parsley and sesame seeds.

Peaches and tomatoes—the two big, juicy treats of summer. They come into season at just about the same time, and a good tomato year usually also means a good peach year. A hot, dry summer seems to work well for both. Given that they are so closely related by essential juiciness and seasonality, it seemed to me that a peach could be treated much like a tomato and made into a summer salad using the flavors traditionally paired with tomatoes.

Peachy Salad

1 small red onion

Sea salt

Juice of 1 lemon

3 tablespoons extra-virgin olive oil

3 big ripe peaches, preferably freestone

12 fresh basil or black mint leaves

Thinly slice the red onion into rings. Put in a bowl and sprinkle with a little sea salt. Let sit for 30 minutes to wilt.

Add the lemon juice and olive oil to the bowl with the onion. Cut the peaches in half, remove the stone, and cut into ½-inch wedges. Add the peaches to the onion mixture and toss gently to mix. Tear the basil or mint over the salad and toss gently to mix everything together. Divide among individual plates, garnish with a drizzle of olive oil and a sprinkle of sea salt, and serve right away.

This salad was appropriated from a Greek restaurant in midtown called Molyvos that I went to with my parents at some point in the late 1990s. It reminded me of our Greek neighbors when I was growing up—extraordinary cooks. They would invite us over for dinner, and even to my teen-age palate, everything tasted different, as if it were from another country. Even the potatoes roasted around the chicken tasted different than the ones at our house.

I'm sure that a salad like this has been around since the dawn of Western civilization, but to me it was new and perfect in every way. Equal parts herb and romaine with a bright squeeze of lemon; sometimes the simplest things. . . . This was one of the two opening salads on the Diner menu in 1999. I still like to bring it back annually.

Chopped Salad of Romaine and Herbs

1 head romaine lettuce

About 2 cups fresh herb mix of scallion, parsley, mint, and dill

Juice of 1 to 2 lemons

Extra-virgin olive oil

Sea salt

You can approach this salad in two ways:

If you are using the outer leaves of romaine, finely slice them into a chiffonade by stacking them on a cutting board, rolling the leaves into a tight bundle, and thinly slicing.

If you are using the hearts of romaine—which is my preference—keep the leaves intact, like for a Caesar, but for eating with your hands.

Put the romaine in a salad bowl and add the herbs—they should be nearly equal in portion to the romaine. Toss with lemon juice and olive oil, season with sea salt, and serve right away.

This version of a Caesar salad uses dark bitter greens in place of the traditional romaine. The combination of dandelion greens with anchovy vinaigrette and topped with a fried egg is not uncommon on menus these days, but it is always good. This salad could have been included in the Egg Bowl section (pages 141–51), as we serve it half the time as an egg dish. Other greens can be substituted for dandelion: chicory, escarole, lacinato (Tuscan) kale. We have this salad on the menu a lot and change the greens depending on what's in season.

Dandelion Salad with Anchovy Vinaigrette and Croutons

FOR THE VINAIGRETTE

3 garlic cloves

1 teaspoon sea salt

7 anchovies

1 egg yolk

⅓ cup grated 30- or 60-day aged *pecorino toscano*

⅓ cup white wine vinegar

1½ cups extra-virgin olive oil

Focaccia (page 36) or other crusty Italian-style bread

1 bunch dandelion greens

30- or 60-day aged *pecorino toscano*

Freshly ground black pepper

2 to 4 large eggs (optional)

TO MAKE THE VINAIGRETTE, pound the garlic and salt in a mortar with a pestle. Add the anchovies and pound to a smooth paste. (If you don't have a mortar and pestle, mince the garlic on a cutting board, add the salt, and continue to mince until the salt is well incorporated and starts to break down the garlic. Add the anchovies and make a paste by spreading the mixture on the cutting board with the flat side of your knife. Continue alternating between chopping and spreading until you have achieved a smooth paste.)

Transfer the garlic and anchovy mixture to a bowl. Whisk in the egg yolk, *pecorino toscano*, and vinegar. Slowly add the olive oil, whisking all the while. Taste and adjust the seasoning.

MAKES 2-4 SERVINGS

Cut the focaccia into 1-inch cubes. We refer to these as croutons, although we don't actually toast them. The focaccia becomes almost inedibly crunchy when toasted, so we leave the bread soft, which means that it is chewy and nicely absorbs the anchovy vinaigrette. If you are using other bread, drizzle it with olive oil and toast it in the oven. We would recommend six squares per serving.

Place the focaccia in a large bowl and toss with ¼ cup of the vinaigrette. Add the dandelion greens and toss with the focaccia, adding more vinaigrette as necessary to coat the greens lightly. Grate additional *pecorino toscano* over the greens and toss again. Portion the salad into individual bowls. Garnish with a cracking of pepper and serve. If you like, follow the recipe for frying eggs on page 63 and slide one on top of each salad.

I became enamored of radishes on my first and only trip to France the year after I left Savoy and before I started at Diner. I was delighted by the sight of piles of absolutely stunning breakfast radishes at every market. I have no memory of a radish before then, though I surely must have eaten one.

I was staying with my friends Carolyn and Caroline, who were spending the summer in the Loire Valley. We shopped, then cooked and ate at the little cave-house they'd rented from Carolyn's cousin (we also ate in restaurants, at the outdoor markets, had picnics, and ate goat cheese, every kind of pork product, and our favorite biscuits—and I gained fifteen pounds in three weeks).

Radishes and Chives with Yogurt and Baby Arugula

1 bunch red globe or French breakfast radishes

1 small bunch fresh chives

½ cup yogurt, homemade (see page 54) or best-quality store-bought

3 tablespoons extra-virgin olive oil, plus more for drizzling

1 tablespoon white wine vinegar

Sea salt

A handful of baby arugula

Fresh lemon juice

MAKES 2-4 SERVINGS

Though the breakfast radishes were mild, in the spirit of things, we ate them with heaps of butter and salt. I proudly put radishes accompanied in this way on the early Diner menus.

I remain enthusiastic about radishes. I can't limit myself when ordering them and must take every available variety—sparklers, Easter eggs, watermelon, icicle, black. For six months out of the year, to take anything out of or put anything into the reach-in refrigerator requires moving a box or bag of radishes. My obsession is kindly tolerated by my partners.

There is something really special about the spectacular crunch of a radish—watery, earthy, spicy. This salad celebrates just those qualities.

Cut the radishes in half or quarters, depending on their size. Mince the chives as finely as possible.

In a bowl, whisk together the yogurt, olive oil, vinegar, and a pinch of salt. Add the radishes and chives to the seasoned yogurt and toss to mix.

In another bowl, lightly dress the arugula with a squeeze of lemon, a drizzle of olive oil, and another pinch of salt. Divide the arugula among individual bowls and spoon the radishes on top. Finish with a drizzle of olive oil and a pinch of coarse sea salt and serve right away.

I could write a tome on tomatoes. Eggs, greens, radishes, shell beans, sesame seeds, tomatoes—they are among my great loves. This adoration of the tomato comes directly through my DNA; my mother and I are in heaven over a bowl of tomato salad.

It could be that bread was made just to sop up the pool of juice a tomato makes when marinated in salt and olive oil. The essence of this is embodied in panzanella.

Panzanella

4 large ripe tomatoes

4 garlic cloves, thinly sliced

Sea salt

¼ cup extra-virgin olive oil

2 tablespoons red wine vinegar

24 fresh basil leaves

Focaccia (page 36) or other crusty Italian-style bread

MAKES 4 SERVINGS

Core and cut the tomatoes in half from top to bottom. Place a tomato half flat on a cutting board and cut in half again across the middle, then cut lengthwise into ½-inch slices. Repeat to slice the remaining tomatoes.

Place the tomatoes and garlic in a bowl and season with salt. When the tomatoes start to release their liquid, add the olive oil and vinegar. Let the tomato mixture sit for 1 hour to marinate.

When you are ready to eat, tear the basil and add it to the tomatoes. Finally, cut the focaccia into 1-inch cubes and toss with the tomatoes. Check the seasoning and serve right away.

There is an idea in cooking that "things that grow together go together." And despite the cute and annoying adage-iness of this, it is mostly true. I like to apply this thinking to things that are the same color as well. Sometimes I approach a dish with the condition that I want it to be monochromatic. I find this particularly appealing when it comes to things that are green.

This recipe calls for freshly homemade crème fraîche, which in the spirit of making everything ourselves and despite what the health department might say, is another of the basics we like to have on hand. Use a good-quality store-bought brand to save time, if you like. If making your own, note that you need to begin it the night before. And as always, an egg on top of this salad wouldn't be a bad idea.

Flageolets with Green Dressing and Butter Lettuce

FOR THE CRÈME FRAÎCHE

2 cups cream

2 tablespoons buttermilk

1 cup freshly shelled flageolet beans (preferably; you can use dried if you have to)

Extra-virgin olive oil

Kosher salt

½ cup Pistou (page 51)

Sea salt

White wine vinegar

1 head butter lettuce

MAKES 2-4 SERVINGS

TO MAKE THE CRÈME FRAÎCHE, combine the cream and buttermilk in a glass jar. Cover the jar with plastic wrap and let stand until thickened, overnight or up to 2 days. When the crème fraîche is nice and thick, transfer it to the refrigerator. (Store, tightly covered, in the refrigerator for up to 2 weeks.)

Put the beans in a pot with enough water to cover by 2 inches. Bring to a boil over high heat, skimming off any foam that rises to the surface. Pour a good dose of olive oil over the beans and turn down the heat to maintain a simmer. Cook until tender, 20 to 30 minutes. Season with kosher salt and let cool in the cooking liquid.

In a bowl, whisk together the *pistou* and ¼ cup of the crème fraîche. Season with sea salt, white wine vinegar, and olive oil. Drain the cooled beans and toss with the green dressing. You want a loose mixture of beans and dressing. Divide the butter lettuce leaves among individual bowls. Spoon the bean mixture on top of the lettuce. Serve right away.

In late summer, fresh shell beans arrive at the market. These are among my favorite things to eat all year. The cranberry bean is the definitive creamy, buttery, savory bean. Its texture is unparalleled. I cannot buy enough of these to satisfy my affection.

This method for cooking fresh cranberry beans came from Toby Aarons, whom I worked with at the Union Square farmers' market (for Tim Stark at Eckerton Hill Farms) the same summer I went to France and just before Diner. She got this recipe from Marcella Hazan (who got it from her husband's housekeeper) and showed me just how she does it. I believe this is the best preparation for beans on record.

Cranberry Beans with Charred Peppers and Mustard Greens

2 cups fresh shelled cranberry beans

½ cup extra-virgin olive oil, plus 3 tablespoons and as needed

12 cloves garlic, 6 halved lengthwise and 6 thinly sliced

1 bunch fresh sage

Kosher salt

4 mixed peppers such red bell, cubanelle, mild chile, and/or Italian fryer

1 bunch mustard greens, tough stems and spines removed

Coarse sea salt

MAKES 2-4 SERVINGS

Put the cranberry beans in a pot and add just enough water to cover. Over high heat, bring the beans up to a boil, skimming off any white foam that that rises to the surface, then turn down to a simmer. Stir in ¼ cup of the olive oil, the halved garlic, and 12 sage leaves. Check the beans for doneness after 20 minutes; they will probably take about 30 minutes to cook. When the beans are tender, season with kosher salt and let cool in the cooking liquid.

Core and seed the peppers. Cut them in half lengthwise, then into ½-inch strips. In a cast-iron skillet over high heat, heat the 3 three tablespoons olive oil. Working in batches if necessary, add the peppers and spread in a single layer. Season the peppers with salt and cook them until they brown, and even char, 8 to 10 minutes, turning once with tongs. Add additional oil to the pan if it starts to get too dry. Continue on this way until all of the peppers are cooked, transferring them to a heatproof bowl as they are finished.

CONTINUED

Meanwhile, pour the remaining ¼ cup olive oil into a small frying pan over medium heat. Add the sliced garlic and sauté until the garlic starts to sizzle and turn golden, about 3 minutes. Add another 12 sage leaves or so to the garlic and oil. When the sage wilts, remove from the heat. Pour the contents of the pan over the peppers and fold gently to mix well.

Place the mustard greens on the bottom of a serving bowl or platter. (I don't like to cut or tear mustard greens, even if they are rather large. I prefer to serve them whole and let the diners cut them as they eat.) Using a slotted spoon, lift the cranberry beans from their cooking liquid and place them on top of the mustard greens. Spoon the peppers and their oil on top of the beans and greens. Sprinkle with a little coarse sea salt. Serve warm or chilled.

Farro is a particularly versatile variety of whole-grain wheat. It resembles barley and is a soft, nutty grain that is quick and easy to cook. I like to make grain salads all year, but I like them best in the spring, with the young green vegetables just arriving. I have made many versions of this salad, often with jasmine rice in place of the farro and with other vegetables besides peas, fava beans, asparagus, ramps. This salad can be eaten just as it is or be made into more of an event by serving it on top of sliced prosciutto or Serrano ham. It's perfect with a glass of crisp white wine.

Farro, Peas, and Leeks

2 large leeks

2 cups farro

Kosher salt

¼ cup extra-virgin olive oil, plus more for drizzling, or as needed

2 cups shelled fresh peas

½ cup Lazy Housewife Vinaigrette (page 48)

MAKES 4 SERVINGS

Cut the leeks into quarters lengthwise. Slice each quarter at a slight angle, discarding the tough dark green tops. Put the cut leeks in a bowl with plenty of cold water and set aside to let them release their grit.

Place the farro in a pot and add enough water to cover by 1 inch. Stir in 1 tablespoon salt, bring to a boil over high heat, and then reduce the heat to medium. Cook until the farro is tender, about 20 minutes. Strain the farro through a strainer, drizzle with a little olive oil, and set aside to cool.

Bring a small pot of salted water to a boil. Have ready a large bowl of ice water. Add the peas to the boiling water and blanch until the water returns to a boil. Drain and plunge immediately into the ice bath to stop the cooking, then drain again. Set aside in a strainer to drain thoroughly.

Drain the leeks thoroughly and spin dry in a salad spinner. Heat a large skillet and add the ¼ cup olive oil; it should cover the entire bottom of the pan. Add the leeks, season with salt, and cook, stirring often, until tender, about 5 minutes.

Combine the farro, leeks, and peas in a bowl. Add about ¼ cup of the vinaigrette to the salad and toss to mix and coat well. Because of the grain, this salad will require a lot of vinaigrette; you don't want it to be dry. Continue to add vinaigrette until the salad tastes well seasoned and is properly loose and oily. Taste for salt as you go. Divide among individual bowls and serve right away.

CHAPTER 4

SWEETS AND DRINKS

||||||||||||||||||||||||||||||||||||||||||||||||||||||||||||||||||||||||||||||||||||||||||||||||||||||||||||||||||||||

Originally, we really thought Saltie would be more of a bakery. We hadn't exorcised the ghost of Cheeks (see page 22) and assumed we had to follow in its footsteps. Plus we had Elizabeth, a baker in the truest sense. But as you know by now, if you've been reading along, that's not how the story goes . . . by reputation, Saltie is foremost a sandwich shop, but we all still include that it's a bakery when describing it. The defining architectural detail of Saltie is the big pastry case; the impressive display of baked goods is pretty much the only visual prompt you have as to what this space is about when you first walk in. The pastries are the gateway to what lies ahead. They set the tone and tell the world that we're not selling cupcakes.

||||||||||||||||||||||||||||||||||||||||||||||||||||||||||||||||||||||||||||||||||||||||||||||||||||||||||||||||||||||

|||||||||||||||||||||||||||||||||||||||||||||||||||||||||||||||||||||||||||||||||||||||||||||||||||||||||||||||||||||||||

Elizabeth has a style that comes from the fact that she is both a cook *and* a baker. Her palate and approach come equally from the savory kitchen and from a Scandinavian baking tradition. As a result, the pastries and the sandwiches at Saltie are on the same continuum. They are sophisticated, considered, and tested until they are exactly how we want them. It is important that there be a seamlessness to the experience of eating at Saltie, that everything goes together: the sandwiches, baked goods, and drinks must all share a common essence. Nothing goes on the menu or in the display case without first being thoroughly vetted.

|||||||||||||||||||||||||||||||||||||||||||||||||||||||||||||||||||||||||||||||||||||||||||||||||||||||||||||||||||||||||

Sweets

Over the years, Elizabeth has taught us all how to bake. Included in the dessert section that follows are recipes from her battered Five Star spiral notebook, which she keeps safe by double wrapping in plastic wrap. Every time I am asked to consult this book, I feel the weight of handling a precious, extremely fragile, and irreplaceable manuscript. Most of these recipes have been developed over the course of many years of baking and making adjustments. While all of us can execute these recipes workably, it is Elizabeth who makes them extraordinarily. She can always tell what went wrong when something is not quite right, or how to improve upon a new recipe. Whether using sea salt in place of kosher salt in the olive oil cake, adding lemon zest to the fruit galette, or splashing a healthy tipple of rum into the chocolate ice cream, Elizabeth has always found the detail that perfectly punctuates a recipe and makes it uniquely hers.

Quince, a little like nettles (see page 49), need to be coaxed out of their astringent nature to reveal the jewel of a fruit that they are. While a beauty to behold and wildly fragrant when harvested, raw in your hand, quince are quite inedible. When cooked slow and long, though, quince take on a ruby tone and become deeply flavored and perfumed.

Like the recipe for Candied Pumpkin (page 192), the method here turns the quince into a sort of marmalade while preserving it beautifully. In this book we use candied quince to make Lassi (page 202), but we also sometimes add it to Fruit Galettes (page 190), use it in place of the pumpkin in the Squashbuckling Pockets (page 192), or take it further and turn it into quince paste.

Candied Quince

4 quince (3 to 4 pounds total weight)

2 cups sugar

1 cinnamon stick

MAKES 2-3 CUPS

Preheat the oven to 250°F.

Wash the quince well, peel, and cut into quarters. Cut out the cores and cut the flesh into 1-inch dice. You should have about 4 cups. Put the quince in a bowl and toss with the sugar and cinnamon stick.

Transfer to a roasting pan. Cover the pan with aluminum foil and roast until the quince starts to steam and soften. When the quince is soft, remove the foil and continue roasting until it turns deep red and becomes jammy and concentrated. This will take a long time, as much as 3 hours. The longer you cook the quince, the deeper the flavor and color will be. Remove from the oven and let cool. Discard the cinnamon stick. The candied quince will keep well, stored in an airtight container in the refrigerator, for up to 6 months.

After years of being tormented by this common typo, we find it irresistible to call our mousse "mouse"—enduring the corrections. This recipe came from an actual French person, Philippe, who was hired in the early days of the Diner as a favor to the fish guy next door, whose daughter he was about to marry. Philippe was an intellectual, not a cook, and this was certainly the only kitchen job he would ever have. A bumbling sweetheart who worked brunch like a champion despite his weekly dousing of the walk-in floor with a flat of eggs or five gallons of pancake batter, he had a serious sweet tooth and would whip up a traditional French confection in a spare moment, when the mopping up was done.

Chocolate Mouse

8 ounces bittersweet chocolate, chopped (we use Mast Brothers)

¾ cup heavy cream

1 tablespoon plus 1 teaspoon honey

1 tablespoon plus 1 teaspoon brandy

¼ cup sugar

1 large egg, separated, plus 3 egg whites

Kosher salt

Extra-virgin olive oil

Sea salt

MAKES 4 CUPS

In a heavy saucepan over low heat, combine the chocolate, cream, honey, brandy, and sugar. Stirring gently, cook until the mixture is smooth and velvety. Remove the chocolate mixture from the heat and whisk in the egg yolk. Pour the chocolate into a large bowl and let it cool to lukewarm.

Place the egg whites in the bowl of an electric mixer, add a pinch of kosher salt, and beat on high speed until the whites form stiff peaks. Using a rubber spatula, stir one-third of the egg whites into the chocolate. Add another one-third of the whites to the chocolate, gently folding them in this time. Repeat in this way with the final addition of egg white, folding just until any streakiness is incorporated but maintaining the loftiness of the whites. Pour into a serving dish and refrigerate until well chilled, at least 2 hours before serving.

Scoop into bowls, garnish with a drizzle of olive oil and a sprinkle of sea salt, and serve right away.

This ice cream is dense and fudgy.

Chocolate Ice Cream

4 egg yolks

3 cups heavy cream

1 cup whole milk

1 cup sugar

¼ cup bittersweet Valrhona cocoa powder

1 cup chopped 80% bittersweet chocolate

1 shot (1½ ounces) dark rum

Sea salt

MAKES 1 QUART

Whisk the yolks in a large heatproof bowl.

Combine the cream, milk, sugar, and cocoa powder in a heavy-bottomed saucepan. Heat gently over medium-low heat, stirring constantly, until the liquid comes to a simmer. Be careful not to let the bottom burn.

Add the hot cream mixture to the eggs, one ladle at a time, whisking all the while to temper them. When all the cream has been added to the eggs, pour everything back into the pot and cook over medium heat, stirring constantly, using a flat wooden rice paddle or a rubber spatula. Cook until the mixture thickens. Add the chocolate and stir until melted. Remove from heat and strain through a fine-mesh strainer. Stir in the rum and season with a pinch of sea salt. Refrigerate in an airtight container overnight to let the flavor develop. Freeze in an ice-cream machine according to the manufacturer's directions and serve.

VARIATION: **CHOCOLATE AND FOCACCIA ICE CREAM SANDWICH**

One day we were playing around with different approaches to an ice cream sandwich and decided to try it with our focaccia. No surprise: it was fantastic. Unfortunately, we couldn't convince our customers to eat it this way; if you've just eaten a sandwich, you usually don't want another, even if it is stuffed with chocolate ice cream. But this kind of is the best way to eat it—the chewy bread, the salty top—the ice cream is quite content here. To make a chocolate ice cream sandwich, cut a small square of focaccia (if you want to make your own, see page 36) horizontally in half and fill it with a scoop of Chocolate Ice Cream.

One glorious year, when I was cooking at Savoy, I had a black-tar rooftop deck. I decided to plant some flowers. This was the first time I had ever planted anything. I ordered a packet of mixed wildflower seeds that were sun and heat tolerant and sprinkled them into a long planter, expecting nothing. By midsummer, I had a good supply of tall, fragrant plants with a lovely purple cone-shaped flower. I had no idea what they were but was wildly attracted to them. A month later, Guy Jones delivered the very same flower to the restaurant. I knew there was a reason I loved this plant! I had, by sheer accident and great fortune, grown anise hyssop. Ever since, I have kept it in good supply whenever I can. It is particularly suited to ice cream and custard, but it also makes a delicate tea and can be used nicely to garnish a drink, imparting its minty floral nature.

The variation on the facing page is our version of an ice cream float. Hyssop and rhubarb are very well paired. When the tart, almost vegetal rhubarb and the licorice-minty anise hyssop ice cream melt together, they form a float as creamy and invigorating as a pint of Guinness.

Anise Hyssop Ice Cream

3 cups heavy cream

1 cup whole milk

1 cup sugar

½ vanilla bean

1 large bunch fresh anise hyssop, including the stems, leaves, and flowers, thoroughly washed and dried

4 egg yolks

Sea salt

Rum or vanilla extract

Combine the cream, milk, and sugar in a heavy-bottomed saucepan. Scrape the vanilla seeds into the pan and then toss in the pod. Heat gently over medium-low heat, stirring constantly, just until the cream comes to a simmer. Be careful not to burn the bottom.

Remove the cream from the heat and add the anise hyssop, submerging it in the liquid. Cover the pot and let stand at room temperature for 1 hour. Strain the steeped cream into another pot, squeezing the liquid from the anise hyssop. Heat the cream over medium-low again until very hot.

Whisk the egg yolks in a large bowl. Add the hot cream to the yolks, one ladle at a time, whisking all the while to temper them. Put the custard base back in the saucepan and cook over medium heat, stirring constantly with a flat wooden spoon, until the mixture thickens to the point where it will coat the back of the spoon. Remove the custard from the heat and strain through a fine mesh strainer, season with a good pinch of sea salt, and add a splash of rum. Refrigerate in an airtight container overnight to let the flavor develop. Freeze in an ice-cream machine according to the manufacturer's directions and serve.

VARIATION: ANISE HYSSOP "FLOATILLA"
WITH RHUBARB COOLER
Put a scoop of Anise Hyssop Ice Cream into a tall Collins-style glass. Pour ¼ to ½ cup Rhubarb Hyssop (page 206) over the ice cream. Serve with a long spoon and a straw.

Agastache foeniculum
Anise Hyssop

Making meringue is an extension of making mayonnaise—an answer to the question of what to do with all those egg whites. A pretty spectacular meringue is easy to make. This recipe is for individual meringues, but you can also make one cake-size meringue.

Rose Meringues

6 egg whites

A tiny pinch of salt

2 cups sugar

1½ tablespoons rose water

½ teaspoon white wine vinegar

Preheat the oven to 225°F. Line a baking sheet with parchment paper. Have ready a tall 3-inch ring mold. If you don't have one, you can improvise—we cut the bottom off a paper coffee cup, making a 3-inch-high mold.

Put the egg whites in the bowl of an electric mixer and beat on high until frothy. Add the salt, then add the sugar slowly, a little more each time the egg whites appear to gain volume. When the egg whites start to peak, add the rose water and vinegar. Continue to beat on high until the meringue holds a 2-inch peak when you stop the mixer and lift out the beaters.

Put the mold on the prepared pan and spoon in meringue to fill it more or less to the top edge, or about 3 inches high. Remove the mold and use a spatula to give the meringues a whimsical shape. Alternatively, spoon the meringues directly onto the parchment. Repeat to shape all the egg whites.

Bake until the meringues easily pull off the parchment paper (this will vary based on the size of the meringue), about 2 hours. Turn the oven off and let the meringues cool in the oven. Remove from the oven and let the meringues dry out on the sheet, uncovered, at room temperature, for at least 2 hours or up to overnight. Store in an airtight container at room temperature for up to 2 days.

VARIATION: ROSE MERINGUES WITH CHOCOLATE
Melt 8 ounces chopped bittersweet chocolate in the top pan of a double boiler placed over (but not touching) simmering water. Dip the bottoms of the meringues into the melted chocolate and place them, chocolate-side down, on a baking sheet lined with parchment paper to set (the chocolate won't stick to the parchment).

Eton Mess

1 quart strawberries, hulled
and cut in half

1 quart blueberries

1 cup sugar, plus 3 tablespoons

½ cup rosé

Rose Meringues (facing page)

2 cups heavy cream

1 teaspoon vanilla extract

MAKES 12-15 SERVINGS

Eton Mess is kind of like an advanced trifle with the definitive berries and cream but made with meringue in place of sponge cake. My mom used to make trifle. She sliced pound cake and layered it with instant vanilla pudding, whipped cream, strawberries, bananas, and maybe brandy or rum but probably Cointreau. If she made it for me right now, I would eat the whole thing. It was my absolute favorite dessert, especially the super-soaked leftovers. A custard-based dessert goes down insanely easy, despite the fact that it is constructed of cream and egg yolks. I am English in my affection for all things custard.

Place the strawberries and blueberries in a large bowl and sprinkle with the 1 cup sugar and the rosé. Let the fruit macerate for 1 hour.

Break the meringues into bite-size pieces. Whip the cream with the 3 tablespoons sugar and the vanilla to soft peaks. Place an even layer of the meringue pieces in the bottom of a nice, big glass trifle bowl. Follow with a layer of berries and a layer of whipped cream. Repeat until the bowl is full. Let the mess sit at room temperature for 20 minutes to soften and come together. Scoop into dessert bowls or parfait glasses and serve.

These cookies got their name from Lisa, one of our nudgiest regular customers (as well as our resident psychic). If an *amuse-bouche* is the French way to titillate the mouth, the Nudge works in the Yiddish way: to "pester" the mouth. There is something wonderfully nudgey about the way these cookies go down—in a dense, almost fudgy, mouthful.

Chocolate Nudge Cookies

½ cup shelled, toasted pistachios

1 tablespoon granulated sugar, plus 1 cup

1½ cups plus 1 tablespoon all-purpose flour

⅓ cup unsweetened dark (Dutch-processed) cocoa powder

¼ teaspoon baking powder

½ teaspoon salt

1 cup (2 sticks) unsalted butter, softened

1 cup powdered sugar

2 teaspoons vanilla extract

1 tablespoon rum

2 cups bittersweet chocolate chips

Preheat the oven to 325°F. Line a baking sheet with parchment paper.

Using the pulse setting, grind the pistachios and 1 tablespoon granulated sugar in a food processor until they have the consistency of coarse meal.

Sift together the flour, cocoa powder, baking powder, and salt into a medium bowl.

Cream the butter and powdered sugar in the bowl of an electric mixer until fluffy. Beat in the vanilla and rum.

Add the dry ingredients and the pistachios to the butter mixture, beating until well combined and scraping the bowl as needed. Stir in the chocolate chips and mix until evenly distributed. Form the dough into 2-inch balls. Put the 1 cup granulated sugar in a bowl and toss the balls of dough in the sugar until evenly coated. Place the cookies on the prepared sheet about 3 inches apart and bake until they begin to crackle all over the top and are just firm to the touch, about 10 minutes. Let cool completely on the sheet.

Store in a plastic container with a tight-fitting lid. In the cooler months, these cookies will hold up well for 4 to 5 days. In the humid months, they last only 2 days before starting to crumble.

This cookie evolved out of another cookie that is an even more advanced and adult version of a chocolate chip. Elizabeth's sister, Susan, who owns her own bakery and restaurant in Minneapolis, made a buckwheat and cocoa nib cookie when we went out for a visit. It is remarkable when you taste something strikingly new in a genre as commonplace as the chocolate chip cookie. We came back to Brooklyn and tried to reproduce Susan's cookie but couldn't quite get them right. As a result, we changed the buckwheat flour to almond flour and the cocoa nibs to bittersweet chocolate. An altogether different cookie, but nonetheless a sophisticated chocolate chip, just what we were in the market for.

The Adult Chip

2 cups skin-on almonds

2½ cups all-purpose flour

½ teaspoon salt

1 cup (2 sticks) unsalted butter, softened

1⅓ cups sugar

1 tablespoon vanilla extract

⅔ cup chopped 80% bittersweet chocolate

MAKES ABOUT
12
COOKIES

Preheat the oven to 350°F. Spread the almonds on a baking sheet and toast in the oven until lightly browned and fragrant, about 5 minutes. Let cool.

Transfer the toasted almonds to a food processor. Using the pulse setting, process the almonds until finely ground. Add the flour and salt and pulse until well blended with the almonds.

Cream the butter and sugar in the bowl of an electric mixer until fluffy. Add the almond flour mixture and beat until incorporated. Beat in the vanilla. Add the chopped chocolate and beat until evenly distributed. Refrigerate the dough until well chilled, at least 1 hour or up to 1 week.

When you're ready to bake, preheat the oven to 325°F. Line a baking sheet with parchment paper.

Roll the cookie dough into 2-inch balls. Place on the prepared sheet about 3 inches apart and lightly flatten each with the palm of your hand. Bake until just starting to brown around the edges, about 10 minutes. Let cool completely on the sheet.

Store cookies in a plastic container with a tight-fitting lid. Adult chips are best eaten on the day they are made.

Flowers can be a potent flavoring agent despite their ethereal associations. When used in baking, flowers are solid and recognizable. These cookies are quite assertively lavender, tempered from being grandmotherly by the richness of the shortbread.

Lavender Bars

1¼ teaspoons dried lavender flowers or 2½ teaspoons fresh lavender flowers

1 cup (2 sticks) unsalted butter, softened, plus more for greasing

¾ cup granulated sugar

1 egg yolk

1 teaspoon vanilla extract

2 cups all-purpose flour

½ teaspoon salt

Turbinado sugar for sprinkling

Grind the lavender in a mortar with a pestle or in a spice grinder. Cream the butter and granulated sugar in the bowl of an electric mixer until fluffy. Add the egg yolk and vanilla and beat until smooth.

In a bowl, whisk together the flour, salt, and lavender. Add the flour mixture to the butter and beat to incorporate well. Turn the dough out onto parchment paper or plastic wrap. Flatten the dough with your hands and shape it into approximately a 10-inch square. Wrap the dough in plastic wrap and refrigerate overnight or for up to 1 week. This gives the lavender flavor time to develop. An hour before baking, remove the shortbread dough from the refrigerator to soften.

Preheat the oven to 325°F. Grease a 10-inch baking pan with butter, line it with parchment paper, and grease it again.

Press the dough into the pan with your hands, making sure it is even and smooth. Prick the dough with a fork and sprinkle evenly with the turbinado sugar. Bake the shortbread until golden brown, about 20 minutes. Let cool until just slightly warm, then cut into 2-inch squares. Wrap the shortbread with plastic wrap in the baking pan. It will keep for 3 days.

I would never have made a yeast dough like this without Elizabeth as my spiritual pastry guide. For years I would look at recipes for yeasted pastries, thinking that they were just too difficult or time consuming. As with so many of the things in Elizabeth's repertoire, this brioche dough is all you need to make the many varieties of sweet morning breads that may have eluded you as they did me.

Chocolate Brioche

FOR THE BRIOCHE DOUGH

¼ cup whole milk

4 large eggs

2 teaspoons dry active yeast

2½ cups plus 2 tablespoons all-purpose flour, plus more for dusting

¼ cup sugar

1 teaspoon salt

9 tablespoons (4½ ounces) unsalted butter, softened

MAKES 10–12 BRIOCHE BUNS

TO MAKE THE BRIOCHE DOUGH, in a saucepan, heat the milk over medium-high heat to just before scalding. Break one of the eggs into a heatproof bowl and very slowly whisk in the hot milk. Add the yeast and ¾ cup of the flour and whisk to combine.

Sprinkle another ¾ cup of the flour evenly over the top of the yeast and flour mixture. Don't mix the flour in; just let it sit on top of the yeast mixture. Let the dough rise in a warm place for 1 hour.

Transfer the dough to the bowl of a stand mixer. Using the paddle attachment, beat in the sugar, salt, remaining 3 eggs, and remaining 1 cup plus 2 tablespoons flour. Once everything is well blended, beat in the butter, 1 tablespoon at a time, until incorporated.

Place the brioche dough in a plastic container or a 1-gallon zippered plastic bag (it needs plenty of room to expand). Cover tightly or zip up the bag and refrigerate to proof overnight. The dough holds for up to 5 days in the refrigerator.

FOR THE GANACHE

9 ounces bittersweet chocolate, preferably Mast Brothers or Valrhona, chopped (about 2 cups)

½ cup heavy cream

1 teaspoon unsalted butter

All-purpose flour for dusting

1 large egg

Turbinado sugar for sprinkling

TO MAKE THE CHOCOLATE GANACHE, place the chocolate in a heatproof bowl. In a small saucepan over medium-high heat, scald the cream. Pour the hot cream over the chocolate. Add the butter, cover the bowl with plastic wrap, and let sit for 10 minutes. Remove the plastic wrap and whisk together the chocolate, butter, and cream. Let cool completely. (The chocolate ganache will keep, covered tightly in the refrigerator, for up to 2 weeks.)

When you're ready to bake, preheat the oven to 325°F and line a large baking sheet with parchment paper. Remove the brioche dough from the refrigerator and turn out onto a well-floured work surface. Divide into two pieces and roll each piece into a log about 2 inches in diameter. Cut each log crosswise into five or six pieces. Place the dough rounds, cut-side down, on a cutting board and flatten each brioche with your fingertips into a disk about 4 inches in diameter. Scoop a generous 1 tablespoon of ganache into the center of each. Pull the dough up and around the chocolate and pinch to seal. Arrange the brioche, seam-side down, on the prepared sheet, leaving room for the dough to double in size. Lightly whisk the egg in a small bowl to make an egg wash. Brush the brioche with the egg wash and sprinkle with turbinado sugar. Bake until golden brown, about 10 minutes. Cool and serve.

A galette is a free-form tart and proves particularly handy if you don't have a tart pan—you don't need one. The galette is one of Elizabeth's all-time best creations. Although it may seem to be nothing new, her way with the pastry makes it extraordinary. The following is a recipe for apple galettes, but you can use other fruit for this basic recipe, particularly rhubarb, peaches, apricots, cherries, or pears. Berries are a little trickier prepared in this way, as they release most of their liquid, but they work well if paired with another, drier fruit.

We make individual galettes at Saltie, but you can make a large one by rolling out the entire *brisée*. It's a spectacular sight at the end of dinner.

Fruit Galette

3 apples, thinly sliced

Juice of 1 lemon

2 tablespoons unsalted butter, melted

3 tablespoons sugar

2 teaspoons grated lemon zest

½ teaspoon freshly grated nutmeg

2 tablespoons all-purpose flour

½ recipe Pâte Brisée (page 197)

1 large egg

Turbinado sugar for sprinkling

MAKES 6 INDIVIDUAL GALETTES

Place the sliced apples in a large bowl. Squeeze in enough lemon juice to coat, using more if the apples are very sweet, less if they are tart. Drizzle in the melted butter and toss to coat. Sprinkle in the sugar, lemon zest, and nutmeg and toss to mix. Add the flour and mix again. (If using berries, add a little more flour to the mix.)

Preheat the oven to 325°F. Line a large baking sheet with parchment paper.

Divide the *pâte brisée* into six equal pieces. On a well-floured work surface, roll out each ball of dough into a circle about ⅛ inch thick and 5 to 6 inches in diameter. It isn't necessary to make a perfect circle, but try to make it essentially circular. Place the rolled-out dough on the prepared sheet.

Scoop about ½ cup of the filling into the center of each dough round, arranging the apples neatly so they are not sticking out at odd angles, and leaving a border of about 1 inch empty. Gently fold the *brisée* up and over the fruit in a ruffled or flower-petal pattern. The folds of dough should cover an inch or so of the fruit, leaving the center of the galettes open. Lightly whisk the egg in a small bowl to make an egg wash. Brush the dough with the egg wash and sprinkle with the turbinado sugar.

Bake until the *brisée* is deep golden brown and the fruit filling is bubbling, about 15 minutes. Let cool completely on the sheet. The galettes should be eaten on the day they are made but can be reheated in a 350°F oven the next day.

The following preparation for candying squash is based on an eighteenth-century recipe collected by Alice Ross, a historian who teaches colonial open-hearth cooking classes at her home in Smithtown, Long Island. She has a vast collection of recipes and cooking implements from this early era and is able to evoke a little of what a day of cooking for a colonial family must have been like. While certainly a full day of work, it seems that the early settlers of this region ate better than we may imagine.

If you can find one, look for a Jam pumpkin. This French heirloom is as big as a baby basket and a breathtaking robin's egg blue. When cooked it gives forth the perfect pumpkin jam, which changes your opinion from *Hunh?* to *Oh, yeah!*

Originally this recipe called for as much sugar, by weight, as squash. That seemed a bit excessive for our needs.

Squashbuckling Pockets with Candied Pumpkin

FOR THE CANDIED PUMPKIN

1 small Jam or sugar pumpkin or winter squash, such as Hubbard, butternut, or kuri, peeled, seeded, and diced (6 to 8 cups)

1 to 2 cups sugar

2 cinnamon sticks

Zest of 1 lemon, removed with a vegetable peeler in large strips

TO MAKE THE CANDIED PUMPKIN, place the pumpkin in a large bowl and toss with enough sugar to coat each piece well. Add the cinnamon sticks and lemon zest and toss to combine. Put the pumpkin mixture in an airtight container. Let sit overnight at room temperature.

The next day, transfer the pumpkin mixture and its liquid—which it will have released a lot of—to a cast-iron Dutch oven. Place over very low heat and bring to a simmer. Cook gently until the pumpkin breaks down, about 1 hour. Raise the heat to medium-high and cook, stirring often, until all of the liquid has been absorbed and the pumpkin has a thick, jamlike consistency, about 15 minutes longer. Remove from the heat and let cool, then cover and refrigerate until ready to use. (The candied pumpkin will keep, tightly covered in the refrigerator, for up to 1 month.)

All-purpose flour for dusting

1 recipe Pâte Brisée (page 197)

1 large egg

Turbinado sugar for sprinkling

When you're ready to bake, preheat the oven to 325°F. Line a large baking sheet with parchment paper.

On a well-floured work surface, roll out the *pâte brisée* to a thickness of just a bit more than ⅛ inch. Using a 4-inch ring mold, round cookie cutter, or plastic quart-size yogurt container as a template (I know I said earlier not to buy yogurt in a plastic container, but I'm assuming we all have one of these in a kitchen drawer), cut the dough into 4-inch circles. Place on the prepared sheet. Gather the dough scraps, roll out again, and cut out more circles. You should be able to get 12 out of the batch of *brisée*. Discard any remaining dough scraps.

Spoon about 2 tablespoons of the candied pumpkin onto each dough round, centering the filling on one half of the circle. Fold the other half of the circle over the pumpkin, forming a small turnover. Seal the edges using the tines of a fork. Make an egg wash by lightly whisking the egg with a fork. Brush the turnovers with the egg wash and sprinkle with the turbinado sugar. With the paring knife, cut three small slits in each pocket for decoration and to release steam as the pastry bakes. Bake until golden brown, about 15 minutes. Let cool completely on the sheet. These squashbucklers are best eaten on the day they are made but can be reheated in a 350°F oven the next day.

Eccles are English cakes made with currants, spices, and whiskey. The English use many of the same words as Americans do in their dessert vocabulary, but often with different meanings. This "cake" is to us actually more like a little pie, a sweet filling wrapped in flaky pastry. The Eccles cake is old-fashioned and holidayish with its mincey, spicy flavor. Very proper.

Eccles Cakes

FOR THE FILLING

¾ cup (1½ sticks) unsalted butter

½ cup brown sugar

1½ cups currants

1 tablespoon ground ginger

1 tablespoon ground cinnamon

1 tablespoon ground cloves

1 tablespoon freshly grated nutmeg

1 tablespoon lemon zest

1 shot (1½ ounces) whiskey

1 recipe Pâte Brisée (page 197)

All-purpose flour for dusting

1 large egg

Turbinado sugar for sprinkling

TO MAKE THE FILLING, melt the butter in a heavy-bottomed saucepan over medium heat. Add the brown sugar, currants, spices, lemon zest, and whiskey and stir to mix. Reduce the heat to very low and cook, stirring often, until the sugar is dissolved and the mixture has come together. Remove from the heat and let cool. (The filling will keep, covered tightly in the refrigerator, for up to 1 month.)

Preheat the oven to 325°F. Line a baking sheet with parchment paper.

On a well-floured work surface, roll out the *pâte brisée* to a thickness of about ⅛ inch. Using a 4-inch ring mold, round cookie cutter, or plastic quart-size yogurt container as a template (I know earlier I said not to buy yogurt in a plastic container, but I'm assuming we all have one of these in a kitchen drawer), cut the dough into 4-inch circles. Place the dough rounds on the prepared sheet. Gather up the dough scraps, reroll, and cut out more circles. You should be able to get 12 out of the batch of *brisée*. Discard any remaining scraps.

CONTINUED

Scoop out 2 tablespoons of filling and use your fingers to form it into a patty about 1 inch thick. Place the patty in the center of a dough round. Repeat to fill the rest of the cakes. Bring the dough up and around the filling and pinch to seal. Arrange the cakes, seam-side down, on the prepared sheet. Flatten the cakes with the palm of your hand so that they are about 2½ inches in diameter.

In a small bowl, whisk the egg to make an egg wash. Brush the cakes with the egg wash and sprinkle with the turbinado sugar. Using a paring knife, cut three slits through the top of the pastry both for decoration and to vent the steam. Bake until light golden brown in the center and deep golden brown around the edges, 15 to 20 minutes. Let cool.

Wrap any leftover eccles cakes in plastic wrap. They will keep at room temperature for 3 to 5 days.

Pâte Brisée

This is our basic pastry dough. *Pâte brisée* can be used for any recipe that calls for pie or tart dough. This version is perfectly flaky and made special, again, by the use of sea salt.

The recipe can easily be made by hand or in a stand mixer. For either, the procedure is the same. If you haven't had a lot of experience making pie dough, I would suggest making it by hand as directed below until you have a feel for it. To make the dough in an electric mixer, follow the same directions; just be very careful not to overmix.

2½ cups all-purpose flour

2 tablespoons sugar

2½ teaspoons coarse gray sea salt, lightly crushed with a mortar and pestle

1 cup (2 sticks) cold unsalted butter, diced

About ¼ cup ice water

MAKES ENOUGH FOR ONE 16-INCH GALETTE OR TWELVE INDIVIDUAL (0-INCH) GALETTE3

In a bowl, whisk together the flour, sugar, and salt. Using your hands, pinch and crumble the butter into the flour mixture until it has the look of coarse meal, with some small lumps of butter. Add 1 or 2 tablespoons of ice water and toss lightly to mix. Continue to add water until the dough just comes together—enough so that the dough is no longer crumbly, but not so much that it feels slimy or wet. (Too much water will make the dough tough; not enough and it is impossible to work with. As this dough sits, it will absorb the water and become more malleable.)

Gather the dough together and form it into a large disk about 2 inches thick. Wrap the dough in plastic wrap and refrigerate until well chilled, at least 30 minutes. Remove from the fridge about 10 minutes before you are ready to roll it out. *Pâte brisée* will keep for up to 1 week in the refrigerator.

Olive oil cake has in recent years become a fairly regular sight in New York City. I used to make an olive oil cake at Diner that I was quite attached to, even though Max, the bartender, referred to it as "hippie cake" every time I mentioned it would be on the menu. This infuriated me—it *wasn't* hippie cake, it was Italian cake! He was totally missing the point, which to me was a sophisticated little something to have at the end of a meal with a cup of coffee. Then I tasted this cake of Elizabeth's and found that while Max was still wrong about my cake, I really didn't know much more than he did about what olive oil cake could be. More than just a cake where olive oil is used in place of butter, this cake is about olive oil, accented with anise and lemon zest, and made magnificent with sea salt. It may seem ridiculous to ask you to grind sea salt with a mortar and pestle even for a cake recipe, but really, part of what makes this cake distinctive is the surprise and delight of a crunch of sea salt.

Olive Oil Cake

Extra-virgin olive oil for greasing, plus 1 cup

1¼ cups all-purpose flour

2 teaspoons coarse sea salt, lightly ground with a mortar and pestle

1 teaspoon baking powder

2½ teaspoons aniseed, lightly toasted

4 eggs

2 egg yolks

1 cup sugar

2 teaspoons lemon zest

Preheat the oven to 325°F. Lightly grease a 8½-by-4½-inch loaf pan with olive oil.

In a bowl, whisk together the flour, sea salt, baking powder, and aniseed. Set aside.

In a separate bowl, whisk together the whole eggs, egg yolks, and sugar until the sugar is dissolved and the mixture is foamy. Whisk in the lemon zest and then drizzle in the 1 cup olive oil in a slow steady stream, whisking constantly. When the olive oil is thoroughly incorporated, add the dry ingredients to the wet ingredients in three additions, stirring each one just to combine; be careful not to overmix.

Scrape the batter into the prepared pan and bake until the cake is golden brown and pulls away from the side of the pan, about 1 hour. Let the cake cool in the pan for about 10 minutes, then turn it out onto a wire rack and let cool completely.

Wrap any leftover olive oil cake in plastic wrap, but try to eat it in a day or two. After 2 days it will start to get both dry and oily at the same time.

Elizabeth likes to use whole-grain flours in her baking as much as possible. In fact, she is always trying to think of recipes that rely less on white flour and refined sugar.

I first had this cookie without the black olive when Elizabeth was baking at Marlow & Sons, and they drove me wild. These cookies have a savory depth of flavor that is uncommon in baked goods, yet they are still appealingly sweet. It was Rebecca's idea to add black olives. Surprisingly, they don't make this recipe salty but instead mellow and caramelize when baked, nicely complementing the nature of the buckwheat.

Buckwheat–Black Olive Shortbread

1½ cups (3 sticks) unsalted butter, softened, plus more for greasing

1 cup granulated sugar

3 egg yolks

1½ cups buckwheat flour

1½ cups all-purpose flour

1 teaspoon salt

¾ teaspoon baking powder

⅓ cup pitted Moroccan oil-cured olives, roughly chopped

Turbinado sugar for sprinkling

MAKES 25 2-INCH SQUARES

Cream the butter and granulated sugar in the bowl of an electric mixer until fluffy. Add the egg yolks, one at a time, scraping the bowl as necessary. In a bowl, whisk together both flours, the salt, and baking powder. Add the flour mixture to the butter and beat to incorporate well. Add the olives and mix until they are evenly distributed.

Turn the dough out onto parchment paper or plastic wrap. Flatten the dough with your hands and shape it into approximately a 10-inch square. Wrap the dough in plastic wrap and refrigerate for at least 1 hour or for up to 1 week. An hour before baking, remove the shortbread dough from the refrigerator to soften.

When you're ready to bake, preheat the oven to 325°F. Grease a 10-inch square baking pan with butter, line it with parchment paper, and grease it again.

Press the dough into the prepared pan with your hands, making sure it is even and smooth. Prick the dough with a fork and sprinkle evenly with the turbinado sugar. Bake the shortbread until golden brown, about 20 minutes. Let cool until just slightly warm, then cut into 2-inch squares. Wrap the shortbread with plastic wrap in the baking pan. It will keep for 3 days.

Drinks

For drinks at Saltie, we serve tap water or a selection of beverages we make ourselves. Period. I like disarming people when I get to say, "No, we don't have any bottled water or Diet Coke." Aside from the fact that we have absolutely no space to store them, buying beverages would be completely incongruous with our make-it-ourselves ethic. And quite simply, we don't believe in buying or serving bottled beverages, unless they are wine or beer.

Lassi

Lassi is a traditional Indian refreshment that is much like a smoothie, but with a little more emphasis on the yogurt and often relying on salt or spice for flavor rather than fruit. Yogurt is a great medium for savoring the flavor of special botanicals like cardamom or saffron, spices that you don't often have the opportunity to experience singularly.

EACH MAKES 4-6 SERVINGS

Cardamom and Honey Lassi

2 tablespoons whole cardamom pods

½ cinnamon stick

1 quart yogurt, homemade (see page 54) or best-quality store-bought

½ to 1 cup honey

This lassi is all about cardamom, about *getting to know* cardamom. So use whole cardamom pods and grind them yourself. Using preground spices just will not produce the same fragrant and essential quality. Use a spice grinder if you don't have a mortar and pestle.

Put the cardamom pods in a mortar and use a pestle to pound the seeds loose. Pick through the contents of the mortar, removing and discarding the pod bits. When the pod is mostly gone (it's impossible to get it all), add the cinnamon stick and pound with the cardamom seeds, grinding the mixture as finely as possible. It will be hard to get a really fine grind, but be assured that the spice particles will fall to the bottom of the lassi and are easily avoided.

Combine the cardamom mixture and yogurt in a blender and whiz until smooth. Sweeten with honey to taste, pulsing to mix well. Serve in tall glasses.

Saffron Lassi

1 quart yogurt, homemade
(see page 54) or best-quality
store-bought

Scant 1 teaspoon saffron

½ to 1 cup honey

In the summer our lassis are made with fruit, more like
a classic smoothie. But in winter, we turn to spices to
infuse the lassi with warming flavors. This saffron lassi
is rich and aromatic, yet light enough to drink with ease.
I like to use this lassi to pair saffron with other flavors
that might not otherwise be in its company. Saffron
complements pastries very nicely.

Combine the yogurt and saffron in a blender and whiz
until smooth. Sweeten with honey to taste, pulsing to
mix well. The saffron will become more pronounced as it
steeps, so ideally, let the lassi sit for about an hour in the
refrigerator before serving. Serve in tall glasses.

Squash Lassi

1 quart yogurt, homemade
(see page 54) or best-quality
store-bought

½ cup Candied Pumpkin
(page 192)

½ to 1 cup honey

Here is another unexpected way to use the candied
pumpkin. The squash is rich and jammy and mixes well
with the yogurt. It may seem strange to blend a vegetable, like squash, with yogurt in a sweet drink, but this
is one of our favorites.

Combine the yogurt and pumpkin in a blender and whiz
until smooth. Sweeten with honey to taste, pulsing to mix
well. Serve in tall glasses.

Quince Lassi

1 quart yogurt, homemade
(see page 54) or best-quality
store-bought

½ cup Candied Quince
(page 176)

½ to 1 cup honey

Puréeing candied quince into a lassi offers an easy
opportunity to use this potentially elusive fruit.

Combine the yogurt and quince in a blender and whiz
until smooth. Sweeten with honey to taste, pulsing to mix
well. Serve in tall glasses.

Fruit Coolers

Fruit coolers are our answer to "What's to drink that's going to make me forgive you for not having anything else?" Who doesn't want a fruit cooler? Like aguas frescas, these drinks are a nice way to experience fruit at its peak. If you want some bubbles, mix them with seltzer or other sparkly things.

EACH MAKES 8 SERVINGS

Rhubarb Hyssop

12 stalks rhubarb, trimmed and thinly sliced

½ cup sugar, or as needed

6 stalks anise hyssop (see recipe introduction, page 180)

Fresh hyssop or mint leaves

Honey

Ice cubes

This is always the first cooler of the season. Come spring, rhubarb gives new life to our fruit galettes and our pickle selection and assures us that the dark season is finally over.

Place the rhubarb in a saucepan over medium-low heat and sprinkle with the ½ cup sugar. Cook, stirring constantly to melt the sugar, until the rhubarb starts to break down, about 30 minutes. Continue to cook, stirring often, until tender, about 15 minutes. Taste for sweetness, adding more sugar if needed. Remove from the heat and let cool completely.

Meanwhile, place the anise hyssop in a pot with 4 cups water. Bring to a boil, then remove from the heat and let steep until cool.

Place the cooked rhubarb in a blender and process until smooth, adding a few fresh hyssop or mint leaves. Thin with the steeped hyssop tea to the consistency you like. Sweeten with honey to taste. Serve in tall glasses over ice, garnished with more fresh herb leaves.

Cantaloupe Cooler

1 very ripe cantaloupe

¼ cup sugar

Fresh mint sprigs

Ice cubes

Seltzer for topping

Lime wedges for garnish

We don't have a lot of opportunity to use melon on our mostly-sandwich menu, but we can't resist bringing them into the shop when they are in season. What could be better on a summer day than a cantaloupe cooler? Here the sometimes cloying sweetness of this fruit is balanced by the brightness of mint, the fizz of seltzer, and the acid from a squeeze of lime.

Cut the cantaloupe in half and remove the seeds. Slice the skin off the cantaloupe and cut the flesh into 1-inch cubes. Combine the cantaloupe and sugar in a blender and process to a smooth purée, adding water as needed to thin the purée and move the machine along (up to about 2 cups).

Transfer the purée to a pitcher and add a few sprigs of mint to infuse the cooler. Serve in tall glasses over ice, topping each serving off with a little seltzer, a sprig of mint, and a lime wedge.

Cucumber Cooler

3 large slicing cucumbers

¼ cup sugar

¼ cup fresh lime juice

Ice cubes

Fresh mint sprigs for garnish

Cucumbers are well known for their cooling effect on the body. This drink is hydrating and toning, neither sweet nor tart, unmistakably cucumber in its ultimate nature. We use large slicing cucumbers because we find them to be the most flavorful variety, and they have a naturally high water content—perfect for this recipe.

Peel and seed the cucumbers and cut into 2-inch pieces. Place the cucumbers in a blender with the sugar, lime juice, and 4 cups water. Blend on high speed to a smooth purée. Serve in tall glasses over ice, garnished with a sprig of mint.

Concord Grape Cooler

2 bunches concord grapes

¼ cup sugar

Ice cubes

Although they seem the very definition of the term "nature's candy," fat, heady Concord grapes, with their quintessential grapey-ness, can be hard to find a use for. These grapes are super-seedy for their small size, and their skins are tough—a mouthful almost too much to manage yet addictively sweet, their flavor invigorating and endearing. We had to find a way to honor them, so we followed the Welch's model and decided to make juice.

Pick the grapes off their stems and place them in a blender with the sugar and 4 cups water.

Processing these grapes is a little tricky. If the blender is on too high a speed, it will pulverize the seeds and the cooler will be gritty. Process on a low speed, letting the blender run until the flesh is puréed but the seeds are still intact.

Pass the purée through a wide-mesh strainer. Serve in tall glasses over ice. It is best to drink this cooler right away; it provides a real jolt of vitamins.

Chocolate Drinks

You never know what people are going to love you for. We started making hot chocolate because that's what you do in winter. Our hot chocolate is almost a warm pudding, a sipping chocolate. In summer we concentrated the chocolate into a cold, ice-cream-float-like drink. As is our guiding principle, composing drinks is the same to us as composing sandwiches or pastry. They are an equally important player on our (small) daily menu. These chocolate drinks are almost dessertlike, showing absolutely no restraint. They have a loyal following.

EACH MAKES
4-6
SERVINGS

Hot Chocolate

1½ cups whole milk

1½ cups heavy cream

⅓ cup sugar

½ cup Valrhona cocoa powder

We don't pull any punches here; this hot chocolate is taken to the edge with plenty of cocoa, fortified with a healthy amount of cream, thick and commanding. A reward for weathering another cold day. Put it in the fridge and you'll have a pudding later. For a hot mocha, mix half hot cocoa with half strong-brewed coffee.

For a whale of a treat we call Moby Dick, serve hot chocolate with Chocolate Brioche (page 188).

Place the milk, cream, sugar, and cocoa powder in a pot and gently heat, stirring constantly, until the sugar and cocoa dissolve (be careful not to scorch the bottom of the pot). Serve hot.

Cold Chocolate for Mocha

1½ cups sugar

¾ cup Valrhona cocoa powder

1 cup milk

1 cup cream, plus more for topping off

Ice cubes

2 cups strong-brewed coffee

Like ice cream, these kinds of chocolatey drinks have a noticeable effect on people, an obvious mood lifter with a bit of a buzz. Who can be glum when drinking a confection such as this? We see it as our public service to keep it on hand.

This is an even more concentrated version of our Hot Chocolate recipe, devised simply to hold up to the coffee and ice.

Place sugar, cocoa powder, milk, and 1 cup cream in a pot and gently heat, stirring constantly, until the sugar and cocoa dissolve (be careful not to scorch the bottom of the pot). Let cool and refrigerate until well chilled. Fill tall glasses with ice and pour in equal parts cold chocolate and coffee. Top off with a little extra cream.

OLD SALTY

Pre-Seaway Salties

Daniel C. McCormick
Skip Gillham

INDEX

ACKNOWLEDGMENTS

I thank my parents, Anne and Bill, for their immeasurable love and support. Jackie, Jon, and Joe, my family. Elizabeth and Rebecca, my business and life partners. Anna Dunn, my long-standing writing partner, who brings poetry to my prose and joy to the process. My beloved David Wurth and Walter Sipser. Doug MacDonald, who keeps me sharp on and off the page. Andrew Tarlow, Kate Huling, and Mark Firth for the extraordinary journey we embarked upon together and for remaining my extended family. Joseph Foglia for generously lending his time, materials, creativity and intelligence to this project, and for his friendship over many years. Juliet Dostalek, Kirsten Fazzari, Kristin Gaughn, Chloe Schwartz, Jill Meerpohl, Shanti Church, Andrea Mersits, and Dana Zissner for their collective spirit and service. Peter Hoffman for an exemplary culinary education. Mario Batali for my first break. Jenni Ferrari-Adler for pushing me to do this and standing by me until it was done. Bill LeBlond and Chronicle for saying yes. Sarah Billingsley and Vanessa Dina for their good work in making this book with us. Andrea Gentl, Martin Hyers, and Meredith Munn for making us look really good.

And thank you to all of our friends who remind us daily that we are not just making sandwiches. —*Caroline Fidanza*

I would first and foremost like to thank Caroline Fidanza, Elizabeth Schula, and Rebecca Collerton for keeping me around and inviting me to work on this book. I have never had more fun than reading, writing, and drawing with you three every Thursday evening at the Roebling Tea Room. Many, many thanks to Andrew Tarlow, Mark Firth, and Kate Huling for the *Diner Journal* and years of inspiration and creative contemplation. Thank you everyone who has ever contributed to the white whale that is the *Diner Journal*. Thank you Peter Meehan for all of the good advice. Thank you Millicent Souris, Julia Gillard, Leah Campbell, Marisa Marthaller, Bobbi Jeanne Misick, Dennis Spina, Dave Gould, Scarlett Lindeman, Juliet Dostalek, Dam Markson, Rustun Nichols, Jeff Hansen, Melissa Shimkovitz, Danny Johnston, Kirsten Fazzari, Jason Schwartz, Tom Mylan, Annaliese Griffin, Hillery Sklar, Sarah Gaskins, Michael Brooks, Katie Chang, Jess Arndt, Nicco Beretta, Little Vila, Megan Auster-Rosen, Faye Pichler, and Josh Whiles, my constant comrades. Thank you Erin Harris, Sven DelVecchio, Mike Navarro, Peter Milne Greiner, and Lacy Lancaster, my family. I truly appreciate you all for being so available to read, be written about, and attend poetry readings. Thank you Bruce Springsteen. Thank you Mary and Carl, Hugh, Evan and Jesse. I couldn't ask for a lovelier crew. Thank you sweet Bird. Thank you Katy Porte, my wife. —*Anna Dunn*

DEDICATION

This book is dedicated to Gerard Smith, whose sweet spirit and friendship had the unparalleled capacity to tease out creativity from the core of us all. Thank you Gerard, for your encouragement, your inspiration and your light.

TABLE OF EQUIVALENTS

The exact equivalents in the following tables have been rounded for convenience.

LIQUID/DRY MEASUREMENTS

U.S.	Metric
¼ teaspoon	1.25 milliliters
½ teaspoon	2.5 milliliters
1 teaspoon	5 milliliters
1 tablespoon (3 teaspoons)	15 milliliters
1 fluid ounce (2 tablespoons)	30 milliliters
¼ cup	60 milliliters
⅓ cup	80 milliliters
½ cup	120 milliliters
1 cup	240 milliliters
1 pint (2 cups)	480 milliliters
1 quart (4 cups, 32 ounces)	960 milliliters
1 gallon (4 quarts)	3.84 liters
1 ounce (by weight)	28 grams
1 pound	448 grams
2.2 pounds	1 kilogram

LENGTHS

U.S.	Metric
⅛ inch	3 millimeters
¼ inch	6 millimeters
½ inch	12 millimeters
1 inch	2.5 centimeters

OVEN TEMPERATURE

Fahrenheit	Celsius	Gas
250	120	½
275	140	1
300	150	2
325	160	3
350	180	4
375	190	5
400	200	6
425	220	7
450	230	8
475	240	9
500	260	10